An Approach to Prayer

John K Byrom

There should be in the soul halls of space,
avenues of leisure, and high porticoes of silence
where God walks.

An Approach to Prayer

ISBN   1 874498 07 5

British Library Cataloguing in Publication Data
A CIP catalogue record for this book
is available from the British Library

Printed by
The Burlington Press
1 Station Road, Foxton,
Cambridge CB2 6SW

Published by
Ross-Evans, Cambridge

Cover picture: Tintern Abbey

Contents

To our son

Stephen

For forty years, John dedicated himself to parish life, and to serious study of Church history and theology. He especially loved taking retreats and quiet days, and became renowned for this. Since his passing in 2005, I have felt that some of this work would benefit a wider public. The following lectures exemplify his scholarship, and his practical approach to problems of everyday life.

Jean Byrom

I

Invitation to maturity

My slot in this course is peculiar. The books on how to pray are legion: much less common are books which deal with why we should pray, and how we eventually come to pray. In my view it is comparatively, though only comparatively, easy to teach people to pray once they have felt the need for it: much more difficult is the business of bringing them to the point of feeling such a need; and this is my concern this morning.

Take the roughly comparable business of teaching people, or attempting to teach them, how to fall in love. What *could* one say if actually asked to utter on such an impossible topic? To those who really knew nothing of the experience of being in love, I imagine one could only talk generally about the human condition, as we call it, the complementarity of the sexes at all levels. But the actual falling in love, the dropping of the penny, as many match-makers have found, one could never engineer, only provide the favourable conditions.

So here. Christians sometimes reach a quite advanced age vaguely aware there is such a thing as prayer, and that many Christians seem to take it very seriously, just as some people reach a considerable age aware that most people seem to think being in love is important, but have never themselves, so far as they know, been in that strange condition, or have ever felt the need to be. They know many Christians think prayer vital, yet, except in crises, have never felt any serious urge to resort to it; and their knowledge of it is limited to the assumption that it has something to do with begging God for favours. So what can anyone in my predicament do but analyse the human condition out of which, in my view, the need to pray, and more importantly, the understanding of prayer, arise?

Like falling in love, it arises, frankly, out of a sense of need. Which means that at once we are up against an enormous obstacle: to say anything of this sort to-day means that, for many people, prayer can be written off as a confession of immaturity. I don't think it over-stating the case to say that the great divide between human beings in the modern world lies between those who believe in an essentially autonomous and those who believe in an essentially heteronomous state as the proper one for man: ruling oneself or being ruled, and maintained in being by another; independent or dependent. The prevailing view is that any kind of dependence, let alone obligation, is belittling and abhorrent.

But look at it again. Look at the case between the sexes, for instance. The reason why many bachelors want to rush off to the station on the eve of their wedding, and take the first train to the north of Scotland is the terror they feel at losing their independence - what Prof. Mackinnon once called 'the footloose ease of the bachelor'. Wedlock looks like death. But if he keeps his nerve, and stays put, he goes through a strange transition. He marries, and submits to the power of love, and in so doing he does indeed die a kind of death, a death to his old 'footlooseness': he worships another. But in so doing he emerges into an experience of nothing less than resurrection: he finds his life in losing it. So that, looking back on his fear in retrospect, perhaps even looking back on previous engagements he has broken out of precisely for the same fear, he realises the full force of those lines of James Stephens:

> **All songs of escape from love are songs of despair:**
> **Who so hath gat him away hath got nowhere.**

2

So, as he gradually perceives himself becoming whole in a quite new way, at the level of the flesh, of the psyche, of the mind, and even of the spirit, she comes to be seen, most mysteriously, as an actual means of grace. And as this revelation dawns, the experience of dependence, in the realm of the spirit, or what people of my age used to call the soul, takes on an entirely new aspect or dimension: dependence is revealed as the way to freedom, according to the ancient paradox, an invitation to maturity. Indeed, dependence of this sort takes us beyond freedom to the point of what I Peter calls exaltation, a kind of equality with the beloved, rather like a little girl's exalted dependence on her father's knee, ruling like a queen. 'Humble yourselves, therefore, under the mighty hand of God, that he may exalt you in due time'. (I just wonder what the little aside 'in due time' meant in the author's mind: perhaps, when we are ready for the heady wine of such exalted joy without being intoxicated by it).

So, in view of our deep modern phobia of losing autonomy, may I refer you at this point to an important essay by David Kelsey, on *Human Being*, in the recent mini-systematic edited by Peter Hodgson and Robert King, under the title "Christian Theology" (SPCK, 1983, p.157). In a section on the Structure of Consciousness, speaking of Schleiermacher's delineation of religion and the God-relation as a 'feeling of absolute dependence', Kelsey says roundly that such dependence 'does not violate autonomy. It is at once a dependency relation on God and the necessary condition of the subject's autonomy, even the condition', he says, of the subject being *'precisely what it is'*. On the other hand, he admits, 'it is clear that a subject's true actualization is not a given. The subject must actualize itself. In that act of self-constitution is its deepest autonomy. The God-relation, far from violating that autonomy, is rather its necessary

3

condition.' Having been brought up on Schleiermacher's definition of religion, I find that profoundly comforting, even exalting.

But I was also brought up on De Caussade, and his view of sanctity as response to the will of God, as gradually unfolded to us through the mysterious veil of circumstance. So, before we go further, may I make another preliminary, foundational, reference to the American Systematic just mentioned, this time to the essay by David Burrell, on *The Spirit and the Christian Life* (271-2), because what he has to say relates prayer so crucially not only to Schleiermacher's general sense of dependence, but to that specific dependence for guidance on circumstances worked out by De Caussade, though interestingly enough without mention of him.

In a section on Action as Response, he criticises the western ideal of the 'autonomous individual' as the 'initiator par excellence ... being a self-initiator. But what,' he asks, 'if such a one were to succeed in these terms, only to find success tasting more like defeat?' The New Testament, in offering a critique of such ideals, offers 'transforming images in the passion narratives of Jesus ... framed to bring us to the point where we recognize how the pursuit of autonomy ... involves crucifying that self in each of us who would ... recognize Jesus to be the *Son of Man*, that is, the one whom our heart desires ... the recognition releases us to a new self-conception: that in one situation (the most self-shaping and significant of all) it is better to be second than to be first, better to respond than to initiate. In that constituting relationship ... the most exalted agency is response'.

The point here, as I hope to spend my time showing, is that not only is God most deeply known in a general sense of dependence, but responded to in the minutiae of daily circumstances, in the energy and wisdom generated and derived in the activity we call prayer, through which, supremely, the awareness of God lurking in our circumstances, is sensitised. So there is no risk of prayer leading to a wrong kind of Quietism. On the contrary, the deeper the prayer, the more costly the activity to which we are led, even driven. As David Burrell puts it, 'to become in the roots of one's being a responder, is, in the words of John, to receive the Holy Spirit. The consequence of that reception is a new receptivity spelled out in the various new capacities which were hitherto impossibilities ... The initiator may be vulnerable, but the responder can no more be harmed'.

For those, therefore, bugged at the outset by the Nietzschean fear of losing their manhood or womanhood through an attitude of dependence, there are broad hints that all such fear may be totally unfounded. We can only proceed, therefore, and explore our human condition, but now without the dark fear of being trapped by mere need into something sub-human.

Forty years ago Nicholas Berdyaev introduced us to the concept of 'non-being', the *ungrund*, as he called it: the idea that our very creation means that we are suspended, as it were, above an abyss of non-being, classically expressed by Jeremiah when he said 'the way of man is not in himself'. This is where it all begins. And when I say *it*, I mean a profound, and at first sight undifferentiated sense of need, and what the philosophers call contingency, which one of them, J.J.Shepherd, has declared is the only respectable argument for the existence of God still left - the awareness that nothing in our universe is either self-originated or self-subsistent, but dependent on some prior existence, the symbol of this being the brutal fact that death itself is written into our very tissues, the realisation of which top athletes can actually pin-point within the narrow span of 3-4 years. At one Olympics they are approaching, at the next they have passed, their zenith.

But in fact, given reflection, this sense of need *can* be differentiated, and I want to attempt to analyse it under three main aspects: the need to love; the need to know; and the need for a sense of oneness with the holy.

I can only speak cursorily, though I hope coherently, because time is limited, and because many of you will already know far more than I about this whole area. Human existence, then, to take the need to love first, is inconceivable without it, anyhow in its earliest stages. Merely to be born is to be exposed to the imperious need for nourishment, warmth and security. But the strange thing is - and this will be one of the central clues to the process of tumbling to the business of prayer - the desiring on the part of the child doesn't cease with the satisfying. Slowly and mysteriously it extends its horizons beyond these basic needs; and soon we are encroaching on the raptures of childhood, the mystery and marvel of projection into and identification with teddies and dollies, and all the private conference with life which this affords, where you can answer your questions to your own satisfaction. Traherne put it, '*our first impressions all immortal are*'.

Rapturous, too, is the fascination with toys, from the simplest to the most sophisticated, each treasured because they are profoundly and intimately our own. And the first suspicion that even toys (and pets) are not the answer to life's problems is like a breath of death to the soul. It gives us the first taste of that anguish Browning expressed so powerfully in Pauline:

O God, where does this tend, - these struggling aims!
What would I have?

All very immature, admittedly, yet probably the first genuine realisation of the fact that we are all basically strangers in this world. But the search goes on, indeed more intensely than ever, though it now seeks deeper satisfactions: friendship, hero-worship, love.

But we have to be careful here. It isn't the eventual frustration which is solely significant, or indeed educative, but these enormous satisfactions of childhood are crowned by a query. It is precisely the depth of the happiness which makes its eventual eclipse so unutterably sad. And what is the meaning of such happiness? I can suggest no better answer than that mysterious utterance of Ecclesiasticus (42.24): 'all things are double, one against another, and He has made nothing imperfect' (c.175B.C.). In other words, these gifts, these toys - which, remember, are worlds in themselves - are little peep-holes into reality itself. 'All things are double': they are at any rate half the meaning, half the mystery, 'something', as George Herbert said, 'understood', however fragmentarily.

It's when we leave this realm, and move into that of relationships, that the feeling of mystery, the mystery of dependence drawing us on, becomes still more imperious and compelling.

The meaning of human love can be read off at various, even conflicting, levels: the production of children; the helpmeet through this vale of tears; becoming whole in the flesh and the mind. But it seems to me that only the poets, and especially the poet theologians, have penetrated the ultimate secret: that the beloved is an actual image and channel of grace, as Beatrice to Dante. Coleridge put it powerfully, even extravagantly, in one of his Malta notebooks in 1804: 'the best, the truly lovely, in each and all, is God. Wherefore the truly Beloved is the symbol of God to whomever it is truly beloved by'. 'There is a religion in all deep love', he wrote in a letter in 1821, contradicting the idea that the love of a human being constitutes a necessary obstacle to the love of God.

Again the matter is complex. She becomes a revelation of glory, as to the child, and hopefully, he to her.

For one man is my world of all the men
This wide world holds: O love, my world is you:

So Christina Rosetti. Yet in the very act of so revealing, she herself begins to be revealed as something less than the revelation of which she is the bearer and he likewise. Beyond sexual fulfilment, therefore, there dawns the realisation that what is fulfilled, in oneself and in the other, is still somehow less than the whole. We are in the predicament of the Rich Young Ruler asking 'What lack I yet?' We are each and all crocks patched up, made workable certainly, like student cars, but by no means what we would be if radically re-made. And so it is, haltingly, perhaps even resentfully at first, we begin to suspect a wholeness subsisting in Jesus simply unknown in the rest of the human creation. So ends our first trail, tailing off, like the modern telescope, into infinity.

The second train or avenue of exploration through the general human experience of dependence I would define as the need to know, quite as imperious as the need to love: the need to be satisfied with what we term truth, i.e. a sense of correspondence between our minds and what we conceive to be reality; not, of course, truth which is mere dead fact, but truth which is meaningful, truth which is the light of life, which lives and saves and prevails. One thinks of that great cry of the renaissance student, Paracelsus, in Browning's dialogue of that name - *I must know.*

Presumably, the will to know is partly a carry-over from our animal ancestry, where sheer survival depended on knowing one's way about. Yet I can't help feeling this is only half the story, maybe even the less important half. I go along with

8

William Temple here in the belief that mind appears at the summit of the evolutionary process because that whole process itself originated from a will which is intelligent. Mind can only result from a process which already has the seeds of mind within it, originating in turn from sovereign mind, the creative Word. This alone, it seems to me, accounts for the phenomenon that our minds are never satisfied with mere fact, but finally only with the meaning of facts, or facts themselves intrinsically meaningful.

You know the stages of human exploration at least as well as I do, so we needn't rehearse them now, at least not in detail. But there are three points at which the passion to know runs parallel with the passion to love. And first, is the business of education by the process of disillusionment. By the very fact of loving we discover that what we loved did not contain the whole satisfaction we were seeking. By the same token, each secret we lay bare doesn't quite afford that total mental satisfaction we were looking for, but mysteriously points or leads to some further conundrum waiting to be probed. 'Explanation does not give man a home', says Lonergan (Insight, p.547). Auden's sad remark applies to both spheres: 'to recount the loves we had grown out of is not nice'.

Secondly, this constant extension of mental horizons powerfully develops that sense of the mysterious resemblance between things, and indeed correspondence between levels of knowledge and existence, which I suggested is such a feature of childhood and adolescence, and which so fascinated the adult Coleridge. Again we find 'all things double, one against another, every thing in pairs'. It isn't that the illusions are pure illusions. The ecstasy which the early love and the growing knowledge brought opened a kind of peep-hole into reality beyond, drawing us on.

And thirdly, a phenomenon new in our day. We are beginning to find some of the best scientific minds placing large question marks beside the passion for pure knowledge. With them its final stages seem to be turning into something strangely different, namely the thirst for wisdom, the ground and setting of knowledge, and the need to know what to do with knowledge. And this we sense with our deepest instincts is the wisdom for which heart and mind are created. 'But where shall wisdom be found'? 'The knowledge of the holy, that is wisdom'. 'All clear understanding', Rahner says, 'is grounded in the darkness of God' (Foundations 22).

Which suggests the third avenue along which all of us are at least invited to explore the mystery of existence, which, as in the spheres of love and knowledge, is felt to be larger than ourselves, and therefore contributory to this profound sense of human dependence: I mean the sense of and search for the holy in the realm of what we call conscience, and even more, the sense of being searched and sought out by the holy.

I don't want to be sidetracked into discussing what precisely this faculty may be, if indeed it can be properly thought of as a separate faculty at all. I simply want to assert that to be fully alive is to be confronted, from a remarkably early age, not only with a sense of compelling moral pressure, but also with a sense of our own moral failure in the light of the inexorable demands of the holy. (Incidentally, on the subject of the authority of conscience, I do recommend you, if you haven't seen it, to look at the remarkable passage on pp 28-29 of Owen Chadwick's little gem on Newman, a tiny Oxford paperback in the Past Masters Series, issued in 1983). For me there has been nothing in human existence so disturbing as the first experience of what the psychologists used to call 'the split' in our moral development, the realisation not only that there is a world - literally a world -

of difference between good and evil, but that the split runs somewhere down the centre of our own being, and that by which I mean our old familiar happy selves, are on the wrong side of that divide, that gulf, as if we were stranded on a tiny ice-flow which has split off from the central parent mass. In other words, to mix the metaphors, the ground, by which I mean the ground not of substance, but of simple assurance and happiness, has given way, almost melted away, beneath us, and we know what the Prayer Book means when it says 'we are powerless of ourselves to help ourselves'.

These three elements, the need to love, the need to know, the sense of the holy and its loss, each grounded in a radical sense of contingency, being dangled over an abyss of what feels like non-being, these seem to be essential ingredients in the basic human experience. And I suggest it is out of this profound multiform experience of dependence that the possibility, need, and meaning of prayer as an essentially natural phenomenon arises for the human heart.

II

Divine longing

I have been arguing that the whole experience of dependence, which we find characterising so much of our lives, so far from being a threat to the rightful autonomy of the human spirit, is in fact the divine, and very stringent, invitation to maturity. So I want now to try to explore these various avenues or experiences of dependence - the need to love, the need to know, and the need for the holy - as possible ways into prayer, leading up to the moment when not only its possibility but its virtual inevitability are realised.

Isaiah I, to take the need for the holy first, is an obvious case of a human Spirit overwhelmed by a sense of the numinous which has taken on the marks of the morally holy. 'I saw the Lord, high and lifted up. Then said I, woe is me, for mine eyes have seen the king'. But it seems to me that the significant point about this classical encounter is not the being overwhelmed but the being drawn by the holy, and the final acknowledgement of his desire for acceptance. And I find the moment of Job's capitulation, symbolic and paradigmatic as it is, equally moving: 'I had heard of thee by the hearing of an ear; but now mine eye seeth thee: wherefore I abhor myself, and repent in dust and ashes'. But the significant point again, surely, is not the capitulation as such, but this as the origin and spring of a quite new experience of selfless desire and assurance of acceptance.

Augustine, it could be said, exemplifies the search along all the channels we're now exploring: with a man so great I suppose this isn't surprising. The passion to know breathes through everything he wrote, however abstruse. The passion to love saves even the most tortuous of his writings from sheer dullness. The tormenting and vibrating sense of the holy and its judgement almost holds the Confessions together: it constitutes their musical key, as it were. There is also, in that same astounding book, the passion, derived from Plato or Plotinus, for a sense of absolute being, and commerce with it. So, in Book VII (xvii.23) there is that affirmation of overwhelming power, summing up so many of the struggles of his life: 'my mind in the flash of a trembling glance came to that which is'. Plato too, incidentally, stresses the suddenness of the vision. Not surprisingly, we find the same passion for rest, in the sense of absolute being, in the man most crucial to the development of Christian mystical theology after Plato and his interpreters, Philo of Alexandria, the elder contemporary of Jesus, who himself deeply influenced Augustine. In one of his works, the *De Sommiis* (I.60) talking of Abraham, he says 'when he most knew himself, then most did he despair of himself, in order that he might attain to an exact knowledge of Him who in reality is. And this is Nature's law: he who has thoroughly comprehended himself, thoroughly despairs of himself, having as a step to this ascertained the nothingness in all respects of created being. And the man that has despaired of himself is beginning to know Him that is'.

But Augustine exemplifies the passion to love, in the Confessions, quite as much as the passion to know. Book X (vi.8) contains a memorable passage which is worth quoting at length, since, apart from its inherent power, it casts such a variegated light on the central place of analogy in his thinking; and by the same token, on what I was saying earlier about the mysterious doubleness of things in this world.

'What do I love when I love my God? It is not the beauty of any body, nor the order of time, nor the clearness of this light that so

gladdens our eyes, nor the harmony of sweet songs of every kind, nor the fragrancy of flowers, nor spices ... nor manna, nor honey, nor limbs delightful to the embrace of flesh and blood. Not these do I love when I love my God. Yet it is a kind of light, a kind of voice, a kind of aroma, a kind of food, a kind of embracing which I love when I love my God, who is the light, the voice, the aroma, and food, the embracing of my inward man; when that light shines into my soul which is not circumscribed by any place, when that voice sounds which is not snatched away by time, when that aroma pours forth which is not scattered by the air, when that food savours the taste which is unconsumed by eating, when that embrace is enjoyed unspoilt by satiety. This is what I love when I love my God'.

As for the passion to know, it is so universal, whether in terms of light. or obscurity, strict dogmatic divinity or the highest mystical writing, that it would be absurd to single out any individual. It constitutes an essential strain in Christian spirituality, ably discussed, for instance, in such a book as English Spirituality, by a predecessor of mine in Swaffham Prior, Martin Thornton. It stretches, identifiably, from St Peter's anguished confession, 'Lord, to whom shall we go? You have the words of eternal life', to the latest instalment of Rahner's Investigations.

Here, then, are the four main avenues through which the sense of dependence can be and is commonly explored. And I want to suggest they are all summed up in one exquisitely delicate statement of Hooker (E.P.I.xi.4): 'somewhat the soul seeketh, and what that is directly it knoweth not, yet very intentive desire thereof doth so incite it, that all other known delights and pleasures are laid aside, they give place to the search of this but only suspected desire'. Which means, as C.S.Lewis demonstrated in The Pilgrim's Regress, that the entire spiritual life, or life in the spirit, can be thought of in terms of a spiritual quest, or in less dated and theologically suspect language, sheer longing. Indeed, Augustine elaborated this aspect of things into the bare bones of a working philosophy. In his commentary on the Epistles of John he says: 'the whole life of a Christian man is a holy desire. What you long for as yet you do not see ... by withholding of the vision, God extends the longing, through longing he extends the soul, by extending it he makes room in it. So, brethren, let us long because we are to be filled ... That is our life ... to be exercised by longing'. 'We are led to God', he says in the Confessions, 'by following the feeling of a certain delight', delight whose growth, I suggest, can be traced along each of the avenues of dependence we have been exploring. 'Man', Archbishop Leighton wrote, 'is made capable of a communion with his Maker, and, because capable of it, is unsatisfied without it; the soul, being cut (so to speak) to that largeness, cannot be filled with less.'

But of course there is nothing original here. It derives from sources such as Ps 42: 'my soul is athirst for God, yea, even for the living God'. Philo makes God answer Moses' request to see him face to face by saying: 'only let there be a constant and profound longing for wisdom' (De Spec. Legu 1.49). Yearning is the basic condition of attaining, as it was for Gregory of Nyssa three centuries later with his characterisation of the Christian life as 'limitless desire for the limitless God'. And we hear echoes of it again in our own day in Michael Polanyi's splendid assertion to the effect that 'worship sustains an eternal never to be consummated hunch' (Personal Knowledge, 199).

So now, after all this labour, I believe we have reached the point where the business of prayer can be seen to be rooted in that naturalness which I want to argue is at the root of its centrality for the Christian life, and certainly the condition of its being practised through a lifetime. I say 'naturalness' advisedly, because you will never pray with conviction, or rather you will never make time for prayer with conviction, or go to the place of prayer with hope, unless you see it as something as natural and necessary as breathing, indeed unless you actually see it as a mode of breathing for the soul. Esther de Waal, you remember, in that remarkable little book on the Rule of Benedict, *Seeking God*, says (p.15) that 'we pray from the same base as we live'. If you don't tumble to this at the outset, prayer will always obtrude into your life as some kind of otiose technique which you in your wisdom have decided to adopt, instead of a life to which you have been, and continue to be graciously yet imperiously drawn, and on which you depend for your proper being. Ultimately, you will drop it.

Prayer is the life and heart of Christian living, which is the fruit of the Gospel. And if the Gospel is to have its proper hold over us and remake our lives, it is essential to see it and feel it as the very law of our being, i.e., the ultimately natural law of that being, the very truth for which we were created, not some alien construct to which we somehow comport ourselves as to some ill-fitting yoke. Which in turn rests on the doctrine of Christian humanism, which states that we are only fully humanised as we are fully Christianised: that Christianity is the truth of our nature, not simply one private option among many - (all very much out of tune with current thinking, but so be it).

The point to which I have been so laboriously working is that the most natural way of expressing the manifold longing of the human spirit, aroused by the divine Spirit Himself, in the experience of dependence, is precisely prayer, above all the passionate, often wordless prayer, that dark and loving intuitive perception, to which we give the name of contemplation, which thus becomes the food of the mind and the heart, and as I said at the outset, in reference to De Caussade, the means by which we

17

thread our way through the labyrinth of our God-given circumstances. Every writer has his or her raptures about it, or, avoiding rapture, like T.S.Eliot, is studiously allusive; and therefore the only thing is to read them slowly through the years, and use them as the food of our pilgrimage.

But of course the point of all this longing, implanted in us through the act of creation, and the action of the Spirit, together with its expression in this way, is that what is longed for is actually attained, though the experience is often of such richness that its description takes us close to the limits of language. Gregory the Great, in his Commentary on Job, says 'contemplation is the subtle tasting of the savour of boundless truth' (V.66). 'When the mind, employed in prayer, pants after the form of its Maker, burning with divine longing, it is united with what is above, and with longing desire, in a marvellous way, it tastes the very thing that it longs for (XV.53). 'The end I have in view', says St John of the Cross, in the Ascent of Mt Carmel, 'is the union of the soul with the divine substance. In this loving obscure knowledge, God unites himself with the soul divinely.'

But having made this central point, and I hope made it validly, two important caveats have to be registered. First this great longing for God on man's part, and persistent searching, is not self-initiated: it isn't some sort of hobby which those who enjoy this kind of thing decide to take up. Both are initiated by the pressure of grace, what Donald Mackinnon has called *ontological pressure*, by the prior, often secret, i.e. heavily disguised, action of the Spirit, by the magnetism of the divine attraction on the human spirit. 'Open thy mouth wide,' Ps. 81 puts it; 'desire of me', says the 2nd Psalm. It is the Spirit of God brooding not now on the waters of chaos, but on the chaos of the human heart, which exerts on every soul this uniform attraction for its proper goal, for each soul to respond as it can or will.

But the converse is also true. Not only is the yearning divinely inspired, its reward is similarly originated. 'Open thy mouth wide', that verse begins, 'and I will fill it', is how it ends. Even as far back as Plato, the vision of final beauty is seen as essentially a gift, granted 'suddenly', as he says in the Symposium (210 D). So that 'everything is of God', as Paul says. 'No one can boast', least of all of his progress in prayer.

But granted the validity of what I've been saying, we have to probe further to the point where the penny drops and all this suddenly, or gradually, becomes a reality, where the yearning soul is actually touched by the divine affluence. Yet it is just here that the mystery is most acute. No one can engineer the consummation, or its moment. Furthermore, I am conscious that there is still something of a gap, a slight gap yet a real one, between our exploration of the human experience of dependence and the realisation of its fulfilment in the life of prayer. And if pressed, I think I would locate this in the common life of the Body of Christ. That is to say, the significant hint that carries me, under grace, from the one to the other is the awareness of Christ himself and the mystery of his being in those around us who carry, who bear, the sign of that being: in the light of the eyes, in the mystery of language, in the style of life, and in books; for as George Herbert put it, *'there is a traffick in knowledg between the servants of God for the planting of love and humility'*. Without these the penny might never drop. This is the living heart of the tradition, the point where the tradition comes alive. As T.R.Glover put it sixty years ago, 'something leapt from heart to heart' (Jesus in the experience of Men, 136).

But again, no one can guarantee the end result. God is not to be pressured. All one can surmise is that if the human spirit, under the influence of grace, mediated or unmediated, desires the taste of divinity which divinity itself wants to give, there must eventually be a moment when, in the words of Rosetti's carol. 'the wondrous gift is given', just as the lightning flash between heaven and earth becomes inevitable once the positive-negative tension builds up in a gathering storm.

Anyhow, it happens, and like falling in love, happens so swiftly we can only know it in retrospect as an already accomplished fact. It is always a case of *déjà vu*. God is always before us. A parishioner once put it well in a discussion of Moses in the cleft of the rock, perceiving the passing presence: *'the moments of vision are the aftermath of his coming'*.

III

Need for prayer

May I repeat that I am at least as interested in explaining how we come, or may come, to a sense of the need for prayer as explaining how we can pray once we have seen the need. And my thesis so far has been that we can approach an awareness of the possibility of prayer through a manifold sense of dependence: in particular, the need to know, the need to love, a sense of radical contingency, and a sense of need for reconciliation with the holy. I have been suggesting that as we explore these avenues to the limit of our powers, i.e. with a certain sense of desperation, we gradually form the conclusion, fitfully and confusedly in most cases, that God alone, as mysteriously encountered in Christ, or conscience, can satisfy such desperate human need; and that the great ache of manifold desire which constitutes so much of our life is most naturally, intelligently, and fruitfully vented in the activity to which we give the name of prayer.

Now, because our life is so mysterious, and our human condition so full of confusion, I want, at the risk of maddening you with qualifications and complications, to spend this and the next three talks, no less, trying to analyse how in fact we make this great leap from questing desire to realised satisfaction. It would be easy to say, simply: well, it just happens. It certainly does happen; but my belief, and certainly my experience, is that the manner in which it comes to pass is in fact as complex as life itself; and that to say 'it just happens' is one of often unrecognised object of that desire, to whom the Spirit is silently bearing witness, and rewards the soul in question by coming to dwell in it, and fill the aching void with his peace, his truth and his power. It then becomes the paramount desire of the soul to immerse itself in this healing peace, by the only means known to man, namely prayer. This fragment of explanation seems to make the original intuitive leap from desire, dependent desire, to prayer far less problematical, and on a spiritual plane renders it even logical, provided, once again, it is remembered it is Christ through his Spirit who is taking the initiative all the time, not we who are cleverly cultivating a technique, and as it were squaring God in the old pagan way.

However, I suggest there is still much more to be said about these vital initial getting-on stages. (This is why I was at pains to say at the outset that it is a good deal more difficult to get people to see the need for prayer than to teach them to pray once they have seen the need). Thus, so far we have been treating the individual in question as an isolated entity, almost ignoring the matrix through which nearly all of us are in fact born to Christ, namely his body, the Church. So I want now to point to four vital clues by which most of us are powerfully assisted in discovering the way to prayer. Desire is a general disposer to prayer; but there are agents which, in the providence of God, can and generally do act as immediate precipitators, thus lessening the length of the intuitive leap still further. So my query concerns the kind of experiences which, granted a waiting, dependent, expectant mind, finally trigger off the desire for prayer in an immediate way, and as it were unveil both its bare possibility, and by way of anticipation, its God-given concomitants.

Always it is some powerful intimation of the immediacy and sovereignty of Christ; but as Christ is Lord of the world, the ways in which these intimations at his disposal reach us are as manifold as life itself. Yet it is possible to distinguish certain avenues which are used so frequently as to represent highways, that Buchan, I think it was, called 'the paths of the king'. And primary among these are the existence and activity of his established lovers. T.R.Glover, speaking in an old book, *Jesus in the Experience of Men*, 1921, p.136, says 'the news of Jesus Christ spread swiftly over the world. Something leapt from heart to heart'; and it is hardly possible to better such a description either of the secrecy or of the lightning speed of the mutual ignition transpiring between human spirits. It was Augustine who said 'one loving spirit sets another loving spirit on fire' So, at least, it was in my own case, and probably yours.

Yet neither the secrecy nor the speed are accidental: they are bound up with the word *intimation*, which is so crucial here. Its secondary meaning is to hint, and it is the hints, not the stiff and formal statements, which pass so quickly between human spirits. As von Hugel and Evelyn Underhill were fond of saying, the mere sight of another human spirit wrapped in prayer may be all that is needed - given the right time and mood - to make the penny we are talking about drop. But of course there are other, and more articulate hints, and it is these I want to glance at now: the eyes, the speech, the style of life, and books.

Dante spoke of the innocent ones in Purgatory as:

**Persons of grave and tranquil eyes
And great authority in their carriage and attitude.**

My heart missed a beat when I first stumbled across these lines, not in the *Purgatorio* itself, but singled out to describe Walter Hook, one of the great parish priests of the last century. For it was precisely such a pair of eyes which, more than anything, finally convinced me of the reality of Christ: still, unwavering, translucent, expectant, profoundly aware, two lakes of light. That 'light that never was on sea or land' can nevertheless be detected in the human eye, the 'light of the soul', as Jesus called it. As C.S.Lewis used to say, 'it's like belonging to a secret society: detect the signs in one case, and it becomes increasingly easy in succeeding ones'. So that, merely by a hint - what Jean Leclerq has called 'a wink of complicity' - to realise the presence of a kindred spirit is to have whole volumes of knowledge in common in an instant, making things like name, address, occupation, etc., so much burdensome computer stuff.

And the meaning of the light is elucidated in the mystery of speech, especially in that kind of speech which tends to be prompted by first acquaintance, oblique, allusive, salty, intimating - here we have the word again - intimating, hinting at the vast verities of God, Christ and the soul, which, for the most part, are perhaps best so passed from mind to mind and heart to heart. Christian biography is full of such passages, pregnant exchanges which also change lives.

On occasion, however, the mystery will be unveiled in more than hints, in profound, luminous speech, carrying unforced and irresistible tones of truth and certainty which exalt the heart and rivet the mind, again changing the whole direction of a life. We stumble on the treasure, for which, without knowing, perhaps, we had been searching all our lives. It is no accident that those luminous life-changing eyes I mentioned just now belonged to a priest who preached the only sermon that has ever carried me into the third heaven, when for a few moments I lost all sense of time and place. Not surprisingly the sermon was on 'The Pearl of great price'.

What a tragedy, then, if I may insert a brief cadenza, that the sermon is now a thing of general contempt, the very name of boredom, instead of the ordinance that the New Testament, and above all Jesus, presents to us, utterances in which 'doctrine drops as rain, and speech distils as dew', the kind of utterance after which one can hardly bear to do anything else but pray, the heart is so exalted. The Church is commonly referred to as 'the extension of the incarnation', though no one seems quite certain who was the author of the phrase. It is a precious truth, which none can lose sight of without harm; but somehow one never hears it interpreted in terms of the furtherance of the Gospel in human speech.

Yet even speech is not enough, considered absolutely. Its witness is sealed by the life. The two hang together, like word and sacrament, each illuminating the other in the manner so pre-eminent in Jesus, who, in Jeremy Taylor's words, 'gathered up his teaching in a few bundles on the cross'. Yet it isn't the quality of the life in isolation which makes us catch our breath, but the realisation, again instinctive, that it flows directly out of the prayer which we see to be so central. This was the root of Jesus' indefectible integrity, a relationship rooted in the Father, and fed by a habit of prayer which he caused them to regard as natural as sleep. All the mystery known in prayer is enfleshed in life, creating a sense of the numinous at one pole, and a sense of homely commerce with divine love at the other. 'Eternity', Boethius said, 'is the simultaneous and complete possession of infinite life' (Consolation VI.16), and here beside one, not only in Jesus, in a man or woman of prayer, is a spark or intimation of eternity, confronting our time-bound perceptions and assumptions. Boethius it was, incidentally, who spoke of the 'right of prayer as the only understanding between God and man'. The Spirit, the Lord of prayer, 'searches, plumbs, the deep things of God'. Confrontation with the indefinable element of austerity which we sense in every authentically Christian life presents itself not simply as a rebuke of our irreligion but as a veritable command to pray. 'One loving spirit sets another loving spirit on fire'. Thus we prostrate ourselves and adore the mystery, discovering it already there awaiting us.

Lastly, books: these, too, can have the same lightning and precipitating effect, catapulting into prayer. To this day, I remember, forty years ago, sitting in a bus on my day off and embarking on the Preface to Bede Frost's *Art of Mental Prayer*. What stunned me was not so much what was said as what was hinted at, and two things in particular: first, that prayer was not simply one exercise among many, but a world, indeed a magic world, entered as quickly, surprisingly through the door of friendship or books, as C.S.Lewis' magic world through the door of the wardrobe; and secondly, the realisation that began to break upon that whole Christian mystery remains virtually sealed till opened in prayer. It was like becoming, or perceiving the possibility of becoming, a new creature. I call prayer a world, and I mean it in two senses. First, the moment that one gives oneself to prayer one enters that realm of which the Creed is, so to say, the blue-print, if that is the right word; and to enter the world of the catholic creed is like entering the world of Dante, full of measureless immensities. You remember Gerard Manley Hopkins: '*the mind has cliffs*', and they are huge, measured in good and evil, this world and the other, and finally known only to Christ.

But prayer is a world in another sense, the sense that a world of literature, first-hand and descriptive, has grown up around the subject; to such an extent that you might say more is known about it than any other branch of the Faith. This alone is an astonishment, and of itself a most powerful incentive to its practice, or the attempt to practise. But more significant than the mere extent of the literature is its essential self-consistency; so that wherever you probe, from the first century to our own, you instantly pick up the drift. You are at home. So that in this respect, we western Christians must be the richest generation of believers that has ever lived, if wealth is to be measured in the availability of good books. And remember that some of them are so good as to be on a level with scripture itself. Indeed, in a bad patch of my life, when I had been totally put off the scriptures by the sheer aridity of current biblical criticism, it was precisely the perusal of the literature of prayer, mystical theology, as it is called, which brought me back to scripture. For the great hallmark of all true mystical theology is its rootedness in scripture. It was the experience of watching great writers squeezing limitless spiritual food out of the densities of scripture, the New Testament in particular, that helped me finally to settle in my mind exactly where my priorities lay.

Never forget - and I shall return to this at a later time in another context - how close reading is to prayer. The anonymous author of the *Ancrene Riwle* in the 13th century, put it lyrically when he said 'the remedy for sloth is spiritual joy and the comfort of joyful hope, which comes from reading, from holy meditation, or from the sayings of others. Often, dear sisters' - the Ancrene Riwle was written for the guidance of three ladies living a religious life together, somewhere near Richmond, I believe - 'Often, dear sisters, you ought to say fewer fixed prayers so that you may do more reading. Reading is good prayer. Reading teaches us how to pray and what to pray for, and then prayer achieves it. In the course of reading, when the heart is pleased, there arises a spirit of devotion which is worth many prayers' (p.127) 'There is a traffick in knowledg', George Herbert said, 'between the servants of God, for the planting of love and humility'. And so I have found it. Nothing helps me to enter into the minds of Christians of other ages than to see, and more still, to feel, how they prayed.

But, as the great Pusey said, 'the English are an eminently anti-reading nation', and certainly a large proportion of Anglican laity still go on in happy ignorance of the priceless treasures so readily available for them. Reading is not everything; but it is still a very great thing. Indeed, it was one of the four basic ingredients which the spiritual life of papists in this country, from the dark penal times under Elizabeth to the Catholic Emancipation Act of 1829. We neglect it to our cost.

May there not, therefore, be something to be said for the establishment at the back of every parish church of a little library of good devotional literature for the benefit of every parishioner? 'One loving spirit', you remember, 'sets another loving spirit on fire'. Dr Johnson picked up William Law's *Serious Call to a Devout and Holy Life* expecting to find it a dull Book (as such books commonly are) and perhaps to laugh at it, but, he said, 'I found Law quite an overmatch for me, and this was the first occasion of my thinking in earnest of Religion after I became capable of Rational Enquiry'. Millions of men and women have come to faith through precisely such an experience as this.

IV

The Body of Christ

May I begin by giving you a compass-fix to remind you where we are. I began by suggesting that desire for God is engendered in the heart by the manifold experience of dependence into which we are all born as part of the human condition, and that the realisation of the need for prayer is reached by an intuitive leap when it is realised that prayer is the most natural and intelligent means by which such yearning is expressed and satisfied.

However, last time we met I suggested it is possible to analyse this intuition, and penetrate into its inner workings, in such a way that the leap from desire to satisfaction ceases to seem either quite large, or quite so arbitrary and chancy as otherwise it might. It is more natural than this, and depends less on the soul concerned than the bare assertion of an intuitive leap might suggest. My point was that all the yearning for reality which we suffer as we grow and explore existence has a moral content, thereby preparing the soul for the indwelling of the divine Spirit itself, along the lines indicated in the dialogue to which I referred you in John XIV. There, you remember, our Lord states that loving obedience to his word and commandments carries with it the corollary, the spiritual consequence, that he and his Father will come and make their home in that soul. So that 'all is of God', in St Paul's phrase, so that no man need or can boast. The initial desire is kindled by the 'ontological pressure' of the spirit of holiness, and Christ, the mysterious, and those over-simplifications into which we commonly lapse as a result of that blurring or foreshortening of perspective which tends to occur when we leave the past too far behind, and conflating into a single intuition what in fact originally consisted of a number of distinct apprehensions, and as it were, broken glimpses of God calling us.

Thus, in the first place, none of the profound questing attempted to analyse in the first two talks can be what the old marriage service calls *'enterprised or taken in hand'* without the existence of a more or less substantial degree of moral sensitivity in the individual concerned. To be hooked, for instance, on the passion to know what is ultimate of itself presupposes an already developed sense of what is true and what is false, what is viable and what is bogus; what leads somewhere and what leads nowhere. To be caught in the toils of the passion to love equally presupposes a moral sense of what secret unnamed thing it is which will and will not bear the whole weight of our heart's love. Betrayal here feels like moral betrayal, a reflection on our own moral crudity for having allowed ourselves to be drawn along whatever false trail it was, while the yearning in us to be reconciled with what we recognise later, if not at the time, as the holy, presupposes at least an instinctive premonition that such reconciliation will of itself require some kind of moral revolution in ourselves.

Such striving and yearning may sound over-elaborate, anyhow as I have rather clumsily described it. But I would insist that it is in fact typical of countless lives, many of them of surprisingly tender years. And my point is that all such sensitivity and effort to follow where the moral sense seems to lead has a result of the highest consequence and significance for each life: it facilitates, and leads to, the indwelling of the divine Spirit itself in the depths of the soul, in the heart, in the ground of our being, whatever your particular terminology is.

St John put this in vividly personal terms in his gospel. And here I beg leave for a moment to repeat some remarks I made in some talks on prayer in a little booklet published in 1981 by the Sisters of the Love of God at Oxford. It is while Jesus is revealing to his disciples the nature of his own relationship to the Father that he lays down a principle about our relationship to them both: 'he who has my commandments and keeps them, he it is who loves me; and he who loves me will be loved by my Father, and I will manifest myself to him'.

This strikes the other Judas (not Iscariot) – who is a good democratic Jew and no doubt wary of special revelations - as slightly odd, and he questions Jesus further. 'How is it', he asks, 'that you will manifest yourself to us and not to the world?' And the crucial reply comes back, inverting the original statement, 'If a man loves me, he will keep my word, and my Father will love him, and we will come and make our abode with him'.

There is no question of special revelations, only the logic of love in obedience. Obedience cleanses, purifies the sight, and prepares a dwelling in the soul for the living God. The words of Jesus recall and elucidate the great dictum of Isaiah, 'I dwell in the high and holy place, with him also who is of a humble and contrite spirit'.

Now when the holy God thus deigns to make his abode in a human spirit, he clothes himself in a mantle of silence, not an unhandsome, sullen silence, but a silence of irresistible sweetness imparting that sense of unutterable peace which made Elijah hide his face. It then becomes the main preoccupation of the human spirit to immerse itself in this silence which is peace and healing, and which contains within itself the whole meaning of salvation. And one of the salient points I shall be stressing through all these talks is that one of the principal human ways of doing this is through the activity we call prayer, so infinitely simple in itself, but so laborious to analyse. A parallel indispensable way, of course, is by following the promptings of conscience in our daily affairs, for whatever follows conscience leads to and enriches peace, which Jeremy Taylor said is so rich as to be a feast. St. Augustine said 'we are led to God by following the feeling of a certain delight', and one of the delights of the Christian life, which our persistent delinquency, alas, renders all too spasmodic, is the probing and exploring of this delightful sense of peace as the known or suspected will of God is followed. Moreover, it may be said that such ongoing exploration, by all means and in all areas, becomes the inner motive and substance of our life, to such an extent that the quality of interior peace is as sure an index of our state before God as pulse or temperature of the condition of our bodies.

So here, I suggest, is one vital clue as to how we make the great leap from desire to satisfaction. But of course it is in fact not we who make it at all, but the living Word who rewards the desire he has himself engendered, and the concomitant obedience he has inspired through his Spirit by actually entering and as it were *instincting* the soul. 'Behold, I stand at the door and knock', he says: 'if any man hears my voice and opens the door, I will come into him, and eat with him, and he with me'. What we have to consider is the fare he provides; and I would be inclined to itemize this under three headings, three courses, if you like: peace, truth, and power.

Bultmann is on record somewhere, I think it's in his commentary on John, as saying that peace contains the whole content of the Gospel. (Certainly it fills a central place in Jesus' mind). So, to assert, as I have been doing, that prayer is basically the activity of immersing oneself in the peace that has mysteriously come to dwell in our depths, is to say that prayer is the activity by which the human soul is touched and grasped and flooded by the Gospel in its naked essence. Hence its daily necessity, for the Gospel is the daily antidote to the daily down-drag of our fallenness. And it is just here, being daily grasped by the divine peace in our fallenness and brokenness, that we hear as we can nowhere else, just what the divine compassion, the *anarchic mercy*, as Rowan Williams called it, is, as also the true extent of our fallenness. It means a daily renewed exploration of what Paul Tillich meant when he said that justification meant 'accepting the fact that we are accepted despite being unacceptable' - where accepting doesn't mean resting in a happy sense of being irreformable reprobates, content with our sin, but accepting the fact that only the recognition of our fallenness is the ultimate condition of redemption, just as the condition of recovery from serious illness is the final admission that we are in fact ill, and resigning ourselves completely into the hands of those who are on a totally different plane, the plane of health, and have it in their power to heal.

The second course in the menu Christ places before us when he sups with us is his truth. Here again you see why prayer must be a lifelong exercise. For his truth is inexhaustible, the first and last mystery every preacher has to come to terms with; his words are spirit and life; a whole lifetime of searching, savouring, pondering is only sufficient to learn the ABC of his mind. When we recall the anguish we had to suffer in order to absorb, admit just one tiny point of his truth, we begin to realise why all eternity will only be sufficient to explore its whole range, and even then we shall be left gasping, like the Queen of Sheba. Truth, of course, can be learnt at different levels. It can be learnt in what we call practical experience; it can be acquired in pure study, both of which it is clear Jesus himself plumbed the depths. But it is also learnt in the activity of prayer, and I would say there is an element of intimacy about this method which makes it unique; for what is learnt here goes straight to the heart, for by definition the heart is wide open to receive it. Thus it enters with an impact and immediacy which is often decisive. Truth acts on the thinking heart, the musing soul with the power and directness of a chemical. We can never return to the state of our former innocence. Not only is the mind brightened and the heart inflamed, but the will too, is moved. This is why Coleridge once observed that prayer is the link between belief and action. (But since we must be careful not to place prayer in a category by itself, this is also the reason why it was said of Bishop Westcott that 'he read in the same spirit in which he prayed', i.e., with that complete openness to the demands of truth which made him obedient to them wherever and however encountered.). Truth is like leaven, like the seed growing secretly: once taken root, it will overturn everything. Nothing can resist it, since truth is the foundation of our being: nothing not rooted in it can endure.

Hence, the third course in Christ's supper menu is power, one of the sure signs of the Gospel, and his indwelling, for his word was, and still is, with power. Hence, as with the other ingredients, the other items, peace and truth, you find a constant and growing longing in the soul to renew its taste of Christ in this Trinitarian form in its prayer, for they are the essential form of the soul's being: redeemed in peace, renewed in knowledge, and invigorated by the risen presence. And it is astonishing how early the risen Lord is able to manifest his power. The mental, moral and spiritual vigour of the very young is a startling phenomenon, and irresistibly attractive; but of course it manifests itself in every age-group, always producing some genuinely original growth or initiative, not least in the curious recklessness of the elderly, and especially of the very old. (I can never forget an elderly lady, on a day when I went to say Good-bye on leaving my last parish, standing still in the midst of her little parlour, and reciting, with meticulous care, a very difficult passage of the Romans and then saying, with profound emphasis: 'that is my Faith'.

I mention these things because we seem now, in the great vacuum created by the collapse of religion, to be moving rapidly into an age with strange affinities with the 2nd and 3rd centuries, when the Church's chief enemy was Gnosticism, 'knowledge falsely so called', in St Paul's phrase, systems of thought full of grandiose phrases, with a pseudo philosophical ring, spun from the entrails of untrained minds - but always manifesting the same feature, lack of moral power: indeed, Gnosticism has itself been defined as 'knowledge without power'. One realises afresh the astonishing range of that great utterance of St Paul: 'God has not given us a spirit of fear, but of power, and of love, and of a sound mind'.

So may I recapitulate. The thesis is that the manifold sense of dependence into which we are born, creates a profound desire for the ultimate: the ultimately lovable, the ultimately knowable, the ultimately holy, and the ultimately self-subsistent; and such desire constitutes the basic disposer to the activity of prayer. Certainly, as the clues begin to open to us, prayer reveals itself to us, by an intuition I am trying to analyse, as the most natural, direct and intelligent way of both of venting and satisfying this profound and manifold desire. Such desire, I have suggested, is of itself pervaded by a moral element disposing soul and mind to conformity with the holy, which in turn opens the human spirit to invasion by the divine spirit, bringing peace in its wake. Prayer becomes the paramount desire of the heart to immerse itself in this new-found peace.

So may I leave you with one last point, the unifying power of this all-pervasive desire. It is only at intervals, usually in the act of prayer itself, that the longing is felt in its pure form, as it were in vacuum, excluding or devouring all else. Most of the time its force is defused and subconscious; it is sensed as the underlying directive and motive of whatever we happen to be doing, as what St John of the Cross calls 'a general, confused, and loving attention', very much on a par with the consciousness which lovers have of each other when apart. We are so made as to be virtually incapable of acting totally without motive, and only this motive is capable of giving meaning to all acts and periods of our lives.

But desire unifies our mental life, too. Our reading, as also our leisure occupations, indicate the thread and direction of our ultimate concern and therefore our ultimate desire. So may I leave you with a lovely passage from Augustine Baker's *Holy Wisdom*, which comes to us from the middle of the 17th century.

'Remember that thy principal aim, and indeed only business, is to knit thy thoughts to the desire of Jesus to strengthen this desire daily by prayer and other spiritual workings, to the end it may never go out of thy heart. And whatsoever thou findest proper to increase that desire, be it praying or reading, speaking or being silent, travailing or reposing, make use of it for the time, as long as thy soul finds savour in it; and as long as it increases this desire of having or enjoying nothing but the love of Jesus ... and be assured that this good desire thus cherished and continually increased will bring thee safe unto the end of thy pilgrimage'.

V

De Caussade

You may remember we are mid-way through a long diversion. I began by saying that for many people genuine prayer arises out of a longing for ultimate reality generated over the years by an experience of manifold dependence: they tumble - because there is often a suddenness about it - to the realisation that the most natural way of expressing such longing is in the activity we call prayer.

But this may seem too great, too dizzy, a leap for some. So in the last two sessions I have been trying to track the flight-path, as it were, the trajectory, of this intuitive leap, and indicate that it is neither a blind nor an arbitrary leap, but one which is assisted, as it were, and like an arch, supported by very basic and common sense factors in the life of the spirit.

First, it is not, as Plotinus thought it was, an unassisted 'flight of the alone to the alone'. Both take-off and landing are assisted by grace. My first two talks concerned the take-off, spiritual desire generated by the 'ontological pressure' of the divine Spirit on our spirits. But the landing is not haphazard either; and in my third talk I suggested we must take very literally the notion of a place prepared for us in the ground of our own being, and filled with the presence and peace of Christ, as hinted at in the fourth Gospel.

Secondly, in the last talk I drew your attention to those factors in the ongoing life of the church which so greatly assist our original intuitive leap towards prayer: the light of the human eye illuminated by the light of Christ, the grace of human speech salted by the sanity of Christ, to whom it bears witness; the quality of human lives re-made in his likeness; and the vast world of spiritual writing growing out of the experience of prayer, whose self-consistency over the centuries and across the boundaries of conflicting cultures, is its own best testimony to its truth.

But now I want to turn to a factor, as I believe it to be, in our lives which, though subjective in the highest degree, is nevertheless witnessed throughout scripture and Christian literature with a consistency which renders it too formidable to be ignored, and which both powerfully disposes us towards prayer and is in turn illuminated by prayer, once its practice has become established: I mean the combination of a strange awareness of God himself actively yet stealthily at work in nature, in history, and in the direction of our personal lives, along with a growing sense of his will being steadily disclosed to us through the peculiar set of our circumstances at any given moment.

There are coincidences - things happening in close conjunction - in our lives so striking as to make us catch our breath and know Christ is near, in our path, like the angel before Balaam, changing the course of our lives. Yet these confrontations are not one-off, isolated events, launching us on our spiritual pilgrimage: their intermittent repetition becomes as it were a connecting thread running through our lives, combining with our plans like warp and woof, making up their texture, giving them movement, coherence and direction, transforming prayer itself into what St Teresa called 'a conversation, heart to heart, with one whom we know to be our lover', and carrying us always deeper into the heart of Christ and his mind, until we come, just as prayerfully, to those final calls and intimations whose name is death.

Now you may wonder what on earth I'm talking about. On the other hand, you may already be quite familiar with this understanding of the Christian life in this world - 'special providences', as they used to be called. Anyway, let me explain two reasons why this attitude and emphasis are quite crucial for me personally. First, one of the formative influences in my life, over 40 years ago, were the letters of the 18th century French Jesuit de Caussade, published under the title of *Self-abandonment to Divine Providence*, the notion to which the first article in the new SCM Dictionary of Spirituality is devoted.

De Caussade, following in an already mature tradition, saw the essence of Christian holiness as response to the will of God as it is lovingly, and of course mysteriously, made known to us in the complex circumstances of the moving present moment, which he said disclose the content of this continuing and unfolding will as surely as the consecrated elements on the altar convey the life of Christ. This, you may think, is putting the case rather strongly; and yet my feeling is, not *too* strongly; because all such thinking is firmly grounded in the doctrine of creation. If this world springs ultimately from the mind of God, then it is likely it will bear the stamp of his mind upon it, in its order, complexity, marvel, and mystery and movement. The world doesn't simply obey laws, which is marvellous enough, but also carries a sense of presence, so carefully and powerfully hinted at in 1805 by Wordsworth in his lines above *Tintern Abbey*. At a lower literary level it is also asserted, as I noticed for the first time when singing it the other day, in the fourth verse of one of the favourite hymns of my childhood, *O Worship the King*:

Thy bountiful care what tongue can recite?
It breathes in the air, it shines in the light;
It streams from the hills, it descends to the plain,
And sweetly distils in the dew and the rain.

But, as I said, there is biblical witness to all this as well: 'I will
guide thee with mine eye'; 'I will never leave thee nor forsake
thee'; 'My presence shall go with thee'; 'Take no thought for the
morrow'; 'I am with you always'; and there is the human
response to all this: the deep dread of Adam: 'I hid myself
because I was naked'; Joseph: 'It was not you who sent me here,
but God, to preserve life'; Jacob: 'surely the Lord is in this place';
the psalms: 'all men that see it shall say, this hath God done; for
they shall perceive that it is his work'; 'this is the Lord's doing,
and it is marvellous in our eyes'; and supremely, Paul: 'God was
in Christ reconciling the world to himself'.

Now what are we saying? What does this mean? As
Nicodemus asked, 'How can these things be?' As already hinted,
thinking and theories like this flow from two great facts of which
we hear too little in normal Christian parlance and teaching:
creation, and flowing out of from creation, what is called
immanence, the pervading of the creation by God's presence,
power, and guidance, as I have just mentioned. The stamp of
mystery which I said we feel resting on the creation is almost a
technical term in the New Testament. It doesn't mean something
we can't understand: it means something we can understand to a
limited extent, yet however far we probe there is always
something further. But it means more than this. Since creation
emerges from a mind rooted in a holy will, the flow of events
within time is somehow not simply neutral. There is a grain
running through it. As Farrer once remarked in his *Science of God*,
'God's mind feels through all the world; he knows of every
nerve: everything is present to his knowledge just by existing in
his world' (83-4). This means there is a kind of grain running
through creation. Everything is somehow in movement. But it is
a grain of purpose not simply growth, so that to go with that
grain brings with it a sense of peace, purpose and achievement,

or progress and well-being, a sense of being strangely at home in the world; while to go against the grain - what the Book of Proverbs calls 'forcing the stream' - brings with it a sense of frustration and meaninglessness at the least, terror and disaster at worst. So that, as Herbert Butterfield remarked 40 years ago, in those great lectures on Christianity and History, 'it is so much in the character of divine judgement in history that men are made to execute it upon themselves' (66) by what he calls 'God's formidable non-intervention' – 'thine own wickedness shall correct thee' (58).

Incidentally, perhaps I should record that only three days before composing these remarks, I was a surprised participator in a brief conversation which contained a nugget of spontaneous theologising any theologian might have been pleased, certainly intrigued, to hear, expressing precisely, though in less elegant terms, this view of Butterfield. My interlocutor was a school caretaker living two miles outside Bradford, whose football ground is in fact visible from the hilly ground where his home lies. I don't know how the subject of the fire came up, but he said he actually saw it, and the awesome column of smoke towering over the city. He simply observed, with great emphasis, 'people can say what they like, but I believe there's One Up There who knows what he's doing and can't be fooled'.

But this is the dark side of providence, its dreadful backlash against those who play fast and loose with any of its laws, however humble and elementary. The other side is quite different, and concerned through-and-through with mercy, even 'anarchic mercy', in Rowan Williams' splendid phrase, according to the great utterance of the psalm: 'his mercy is over all his works'. But how precisely does it work?

To try to be specific - though this is hard, for the Lord is always like an atomic particle, too swift to pin down, always stealthy, always revealing what he has done because we were too slow to see him actually doing it - we might begin with the word 'miracle'. The Concise OED defines it as 'something marvellous in nature', which I take to mean not something freakish, but something which is in a sense a natural fact or phenomenon, but happening in such surprising, astonishing, breath-taking conjunction with events or crises in our lives as to strike us as a kind of revelation, an actual, though fleeting, unveiling of the face of Christ. Take the Exodus as a prime example. The winter of 1953 taught us that there is nothing odd about sustained wind blowing huge masses of sea water considerable distances over land. (I recently spent a brief holiday in a chalet whose lounge was washed away in that disaster). So there would have been nothing extraordinary in a combination of low tide and sustained wind baring the bed of that part of the Red Sea which is called on the maps The Sea of Reeds. But what *was* so extraordinary, and so completely unpredictable, was the fact of this happening just as the children of Israel, that rabble of Jewish slaves, arrived on the scene, desperate for a way of escape from their pursuers. Even more extraordinary was the turn of the tide and the wind just as the Israelites got across and just in time to trap the Egyptians. You can perhaps see better what I mean if I say that had you watched the whole business from a helicopter your reaction would probably have been a gasp of surprise: what incredible luck! But had you been a desperate Israelite on the ground, struggling through the wet sand, as in the traditional nightmare, your reaction would have been quite different: 'my God, how marvellous', the sort of reaction you hear reverberating all through the Old Testament, and the reaction to the resurrection you hear reverberating all through the New, though of course the two events are not strictly on a par. One of the classic statements on the Exodus occurs in Ez. 20.10: 'I revealed myself to them by bringing Israel out of Egypt', and prophets like Isaiah are full of hints in the same vein; revelation through action, however, not in a vacuum, but in a highly significant situation, cosmic, national, communal or personal, and interpreted as purposeful by those involved.

So where does this take us? I think we might well return to Herbert Butterfield to notice a remark of his which has an important bearing on the whole concept of God in events: 'I am unable', he said, 'to see how a man can find the hand of God in secular history, unless he has first found that he has an assurance of it in his personal experience'. So we are compelled to ask, how do we in fact become aware of God's presence and interaction with events at the very private level we are talking about? I can only suggest it is largely through an instinct for what one might call 'the fitting'. St Paul once committed himself to a huge generalisation of a moral nature: 'whatsoever a man sows, that shall he reap', and it is the gradual proving of this on our heartstrings which more than anything precipitates, develops, a sense of intuitive rapport with a living God whose word is sharper, and quicker, than any two-edged sword.

And this, again, at two levels: judgement and blessing. The rebukes conveyed in the things that befall us, are so stern, so swift, and so crushing, but withal so absolutely right, so fitting, that, like David, we gasp and capitulate instantly. But equally the blessings are likewise so swift, or if not swift, so abundant, so inordinate, so anarchic, so far beyond our deserts, that we have no breath left in us. Either way the result is a knowledge of God in Christ on a level of intimacy that can only be described by Jesus' own precious word, friendship, remembering how very deep are the overtones this carries in his vocabulary. And either way the result is a precipitation towards and into prayer of a wholly new kind, whose presupposition is a closeness in the spirit which cannot be described in terms less intimate than union, where the sense of it subsisting in the soul is an inner sustenance, food to the spirit, whose interruption through sin is an agony.

Which brings us in turn to the main point: our prayer ceases to be an abstract exercise, a mere flat repetition of a formula, like the tablets, twice daily, and becomes a dialogue not only with a God known now to be living and holy and terrible in his purposeful energy, but as it were an ongoing engagement, a kind of dance almost, participating in that purpose. So that we can truly say, not simply that we pray or prayed, but 'I made my prayer unto thee in an acceptable time'. In other words, God deigns to be involved in our affairs, not to make life interesting or intriguing for us, but because it is through created clock-time alone that he can achieve his purpose of bringing personality, and beyond that, a people for his own possession, to birth. And because this is a vast matter, there is a sense of urgency about it, indeed about all time. Each moment comes to have a significance. And our prayers begin to reflect this sense of urgency. We feel anew the force of that word to Moses, 'be thou ready early in the morning'. We can't get to the place of prayer quickly enough to 'hear what the Lord God will say concerning us'. We see the point of that maxim of Thomas à Kempis: 'in the morning fix thy good purpose, and in the evening, examine thy ways. To plunge into something so momentous as a new day without taking our bearings in prayer, and refreshing ourselves there in the wells of salvation, is a kind of hubris, unthinkable; for if we do, we have no direction or mental food or stamina for the day: we are clanging brasses, mercenaries without orders or equipment. Each day, and each part of each day has its tasks, and the will of God at one moment is not the same as his will at another. We have to remember that wise saying of the author of the *Ancrene Riwle*, 'she that will not do a thing when she may, will find that she may not when she would'. Each hour becomes in a new sense what Paul called 'the accepted time'; and to let it pass with the will of God undone may mean that the chance to do it may never return. We seek repentance with tears, but do not find it. The time has gone.

One of the great distinguishing marks of the Christian life is the sense of invitation which obtrudes upon us from the moment of waking to the moment of collapsing back on the pillow, in such a way that, as I have hinted, to respond to such invitation feels like going with the grain and the stream and getting somewhere, or being carried somewhere, resisting it like wandering off into the ultimate lostness of outer space. The result being that as prayer receives a new stimulus as all this is gradually realised, so the activity of prayer more than anything in turn heightens the awareness of God at work in the interstices of our world, together with our capacity to respond to his promptings. Such prayer develops a new sense both of what the Spirit is calling for, and where he is likely to be found in his secret work; and all our sanctity is in responding in the power of grace.

VI

The Liturgy

Before I get into what I want to say this evening, let me confuse you by making two contradictory statements, to help you to realise how large this business of prayer really is, and how rich beyond any idea I can hope to give you of it. First, in line with, and summing up what I've been saying in the past three talks, let me draw your attention to the fact that Andrew Louth, an Oxford don, in his remarkable book, *Discerning the Mystery*, says, quite simply, 'we learn how to pray from others' (94). But only an hour before I came to write these remarks I began to read Anthony Bloom's little book, *School for Prayer*, which, as you will know, begins with a long and remarkable interview between himself and Timothy Wilson. First, what Bloom has to say about the way he became a Christian strongly confirms what I was trying to work out in our first two talks, namely that 'we come to God by following the feeling of a certain delight', (in Augustine's great phrase), from a growing sense of dependence on a growing sense of something ultimately real behind the changing appearance of things. In Bloom's case, the sense of desire was sparked off by going to hear a priest talk to his Youth Club about Christianity generally. Being violently anti-Christian at the time, he went most reluctantly, merely out of loyalty to the club, to make up a quorum. 'I didn't intend to listen', he said. 'But my ears pricked up. I became more and more indignant. I saw a vision of Christ and Christianity that was profoundly repulsive to me. I hurried home to check the truth of what he had been saying. I started to read St Mark's Gospel (being the shortest) ... before I reached the third chapter, I suddenly became aware that on the other side of my desk there was a presence. And the certainty was so strong that it was Christ standing there that it has never left me'. That I find authentic.

But when Bloom and Wilson came to discuss prayer, Bloom presented a picture quite contradictory to what I've been suggesting, and you ought to hear it. 'The day when God is absent, when he is silent that is the beginning of prayer. Not when we have a lot to say, but when we say to God, "I can't live without you, why are you so cruel, so silent?" This knowledge that we must find or die - *that* makes us break through to the place where we are in the Presence. If we listen to what our hearts know of love and longing, and are never afraid to despair, we find that victory is always there the other side of it. In a way despair is at the centre of things - if only we are prepared to go through it'.

That I find impressive as well as authentic; and perhaps, on second thoughts, it isn't really so contrary to what I began with, except that perhaps you could say it pushes the longing desire I was talking about to the point of despair, which is certainly right.

And maybe this is the point of connection with what I want to say this evening, to complete the long diversion I've been taking you through in order to help you see your way a little more clearly along the path of that great intuitive leap I originally talked about, between desire generated in a manifold sense of dependence and its fulfilment in prayer. For the fact is there is one more place where longing may reach the point of despair and be fulfilled through the body of Christ: I mean the Liturgy. St Francis trod this particular path. Blowing in late to mass - maybe as his careless custom was - he was hit between the eyes by the words of the Gospel. But these words were already known to him: why their sudden unwonted impact under these particular circumstances? I think the answer lies in the fact that what is being said is the object of concentration by everyone present. But it must have been more than this. We all know the horror of arriving late at a large assembly at a quiet moment, in full view of everyone present, and usually tripping stupidly over the first obstacle in our path: but that little nightmare is intensified to the nth degree, when, as happened sometimes at school, we discover that what is being said is addressed specifically to ourselves. This is the word within the word, of which the reformers have given such an illuminating account, the word becoming active and sharper than any two-edged sword. The Book of Ecclesiasticus warns us against attempting precisely what Francis was attempting: 'say not, I shall never be remembered (noticed) among so many people'. We can't hide from God either behind the warm fug of a crowded dance-hall, or behind the comforting anonymity of statistics.

But I suspect that even this doesn't adequately explain why Francis was so stunned that fateful morning. I believe the root of it stems from the fact so many of us have taken for granted for so long we have ceased to notice it: the fact that the Eucharist is at the heart of the Christian tradition, which in turn is primarily a way of life, not a set of words or dogmas, or a mere ritual.

Imagine yourself - what you may yourself once have been, a curious, half-sceptical onlooker at a modern Eucharist, having blown in to try to discover a bit more of what this Christian 'thing' is about. What would strike you about the average Eucharist? First, I think, the lack of fuss. No one would be surprised to see you. When you entered you would notice people making some sort of obeisance towards the altar, with a gesture of familiar affection, if that makes sense. Then you would be offered books, one containing the liturgy, one containing hymns. You would, along with others, slowly saunter to a seat. The others, you would notice, at this point subside into an attitude of prayer, making the sign of the cross as they do so. And then you become aware of a growing feeling of expectancy, somehow shared by all present, fed by a number of people going purposefully about their business in and around the sanctuary, or the altar, wherever that is, until, after the tinkle of small bell, a priest would appear, usually accompanied by acolytes carrying candles, servers, and perhaps preceded by a choir.

Proceedings might begin with the singing of a hymn, announced or otherwise, rather more impressive if not announced. In this case, you would once more be struck by the feeling of a common mind somehow activating those present. As you concentrated on what you were supposed to be singing you might well be impressed by the quality of the language in which the hymn was couched, perhaps fine verse, perhaps profound theology, perhaps even fine music too.

When you tried to analyse the drift of the language, several facts would perhaps have struck you: the accents of unreserved, uninhibited, total worship, offering all life to God; but then beginning to particularise about Christ, through whom he had acted decisively for the benefit of the race.

Abruptly, the hymn ends, and the spoken word takes over. Again there is the same lack of fuss, so much so, in fact, that you may well find yourself obliged to ask your neighbour where precisely in the book the words are to be found, since everyone else seems to be following them. Whether these come from a 16th or 20th century book, your fellow-worshippers seem quietly absorbed and following their drift. Quite soon, if it is the modern book you are using, after a densely worded formal prayer called a Collect, you embark on a series of readings, all of which, you may notice, somehow seem to hang together both with the sense of the Collect and each other. They may however, be interrupted by a psalm or a hymn, which you notice also seems to chime in with the general tenor. For the last of the readings the congregation stands and listens with marked attention.

And then comes the sermon, not perhaps a familiar experience, if you happen to be a 20th century enquirer, rather than, say, a 3rd century catechumen. You may experience a vague sense of alarm at the thought. But before the man, or, surprisingly, the woman gets going, you are partly confused and partly intrigued by a series of notices relating to forthcoming events or current concerns. Some of these are of obvious importance, concerned with participation in national appeals, or whatever; some, of a domestic nature. Included in these would be mention of worship on days of special importance during the coming week, notices of meetings for study, or to hear talks, and so on. Again you would be struck by the curiously quiet unanimity about the acceptance of all this - part of the set-up, you judge - the way they do things, the way of life.

But now the preacher is under way. He or she may begin by picking up a remark in one of the readings you have just heard, and then breaking it down into its particular implications and ramifications. Here again, a surprising fact: the preacher's authority to say such things, some of them rather stern, so you feel, are accepted implicitly. More surprising still is the preacher's own implicit acceptance in turn of the final authority of the scripture being analysed. Other pieces of it are invoked sometimes to emphasise the point being made. But then another fact begins to make itself plain: all the scripture, and all the subsidiary reasoning brought into play to support it, are clearly directed to the presentation of the central figure of Christ, considered both as an historical personage and as a currently living and dynamic figure, and the way of life commended to us by him in the scriptures just alluded to.

But at this point the sermon ends, and leaves you, perhaps, hanging a little in the air, rather wondering what must follow. What actually follows is the saying or singing, with some gusto in either case very often, of a Creed, a Credo, the central portion of which concerns the same Christ to whom the preacher has just been bearing witness. But here the phrases are obviously old, and dense, of enormous significance, and finely polished. You recognise them as one of the universal possessions of world-wide Christendom, deriving, if your memory serves you, from as long ago as the fourth century. It ends with an obviously intended climax, with a startling phrase, 'the life of the world to come'. This comes as powerful confirmation of a suspicion already beginning to form, that what you are participating in is in fact not so much a ritual as itself a way of life, a life for this current existence, with which 'the life of the world to come' is somehow mysteriously continuous.

But now comes another abrupt change of direction. Looking back, you realise the Creed has been the climax of a gradually intensifying witness to the Christ who is known as Lord. Now there is a change of mood as well as direction. The God, somehow known and worshipped in Christ, is now approached with a new kind of intimacy in public prayer, which you may well find conducted by a member of the congregation. Properly done, you may well find this an impressive experience, evincing a remarkable comprehension of the manner in which the Christian way so far concentrated on is seen to be related to the needs of the world and the church at large, oscillating moreover between the most general and the most immediate domestic concerns.

And now as further change occurs, for which you may well find yourself unprepared: a direct appeal is suddenly made to your conscience, to examine it and admit your failures in thought, word, deed, and omission. But you may notice an odd fact about the words in which the priest, who has now taken over, invites you to bare your soul: he says, in one of the forms used, echoing that of the 16th century, 'let us draw near with a true heart, in full assurance of faith'. Here is more than a way of life, understood simply as a mutually accepted custom: this is a movement of the spirit into the actual life of the Being worshipped, who in this case is described as 'a great high priest who has passed into the heavens'.

The confession, however, is not apparently suggested as a mere exercise for the soul: it is followed by an actual proclamation of forgiveness by the same Christ to whom the confession has been made. But this is now followed by another corporate act, which picks up and greatly reinforces the sense of movement initiated by the invitation to confession: 'We do not presume to come' - to come to what? - 'this thy table, merciful Lord, trusting in our own righteousness, but in thy manifold and great mercies. We are not worthy so much as to gather up the crumbs under thy table'. This is the great new fact: it is an altar-table to which we are drawing near.

But now comes another unexpected turn: everyone stands while the priest makes a formal gesture of peace towards the congregation, to which, almost certainly, they respond by offering a handshake to each other, even an affectionate hug. The implication is unmistakable. We are looking now, intently, towards the central altar. This 'sign of peace,' as it is called, you perceive by a kind of instinct, is more than a friendly gesture: it feels more like a pass-word, a check-point: no proceeding beyond this point for the unauthorised. And here you feel profoundly *un*authorised, 'out of it', you might say, lost, on your own.

And the feeling is only intensified by what follows: the sense of movement you are now conscious of is now intensified by watching members of the congregation carrying bread and wine, and gifts of money, seriously yet happily, towards the altar, where they are solemnly received and then offered. All attention is obviously now here. Acolytes, servers, assistant ministers, gather round the priest in charge who then offers the congregation a further formal salutation, which is instantly acknowledged: he bids them lift up their hearts to the Lord, which they do. And now, like a solo instrumentalist, he embarks on a great cadenza, rehearsing the works of Christ in the saving of the world and the creation of a new people for God. But then, in a moment, he seems to return to the main theme, and concentrates exclusively on his last acts on earth, the taking and blessing of bread and wine to be vehicles of his sacrificed life, life deliberately surrendered in public crucifixion. We, too, bless the elements before him, in Christ's own words; and when blessed, he presents them again to God, but this time as the great memorial of that earth-changing event, asking that as we consume them in the Lord's memory, in the presence of the divine majesty, we may be filled with grace and heavenly blessing. The people make the prayer their own with a determined 'Amen'.

Feeling is now on a high plateau, the congregation not simply attending to the altar, but obviously, in a proleptic sense, already there. The priest ceremonially breaks his wafer of bread as a complex sign of the breaking of Christ's body, and his making it available to the world; but also as a renewed sign of our unity, since we all share in the one bread. Prayer is briefly made to Christ as sacrificed Lamb of God and sin-bearer, and the penultimate climax comes in the Lord's Prayer, every word of it 'dynamite', as a Jesuit once said, bringing the Kingdom of Heaven down upon our heads into this very world of ours.

And now a considerable pause of high suspense; all at the altar in profound and loving concentration on the mysterious fare set there before them. It is a silence that can be felt. Suddenly, it is broken by the priest communicating, as the phrase is, then distributing to those around him, all in attitudes of deep reverence, and finally inviting the congregation at large, who then, with nervous yet delighted eagerness, respond, leaving you, the observer, painfully high and dry. You feel you have no business here, and yet something tells you you want to have some business here, and you deeply desire to be included in what has now slowly been revealed to you in word, gesture, and symbol as a complex mystery, as nothing less than the presence and life of Christ reverberating through his people, actually incorporating them into itself, cleansing the world like a river through time.

And this may well, as it has been for thousands, prove the point of your own precipitation into the mystery of prayer, and through it, into the mystery of Christ crucified and ascended. In that lovely line of Berkeley Noel, '*each is himself by universal grace*'.

This is what I mean, and what Andrew Louth meant, by saying 'we learn how to pray from others'. As Paul put it, 'the grace of God has dawned upon the world, and you have caught its life'. As we have been talking loosely about trajectory, you might almost say, using a current analogy, that you, individually, have been launched into the orbit of prayer in the power, almost on the back, of the prayer of Christ's body experienced in the liturgy, much as a space-shuttle on the back of a parent rocket.

That is crudely put. Better to return to the liturgy itself, because I think perhaps the most powerful incentive to prayer on your own account might come through listening to the final thanksgiving: It is the finest piece of prose in the new liturgy:

'Father of all, we give you thanks and praise, that when we are still far off you met us in your Son and brought us home. Dying and living, he declared your love, gave us grace, and opened the gate of glory. May we who share Christ's body live his risen life; we who drink his cup bring life to others; we whom the Spirit lights give light to the world. Keep us firm in the hope that you have set before us, so we and all your children shall be free, and the whole earth live to praise your name; through Jesus Christ our Lord.'

Somehow, the Desire of all nations has taken you captive, and made you an instrument of his Spirit.

VII

Main Crises

May I begin, for the sake of maintaining at least a vestige of a sense of direction, with a general résumé of the ground we have tried to cover so far, and then use this as a springboard for further exploration.

I began with two talks suggesting that we gradually or suddenly come to realise the need for and the possibility of prayer as a result of what is commonly, and often a largely subconscious and protracted exploration of the sense of dependence: the need to know, and know what is absolute; the need to love, and love what is ultimate; the sense of utter contingency, and the sense of the need to be reconciled with what we have slowly come to recognise as the holy. All this leads to the point where, first, we become profoundly aware that the ultimate we are seeking in knowledge, in love, in the holy, and in the self-subsistent, is God, whether or not, and to what extent, at this particular stage, we have so far been able to grasp his embodiment in the person of Jesus. Secondly, we are led, not of course purely by thought, but by the ongoing crises of life, too, to the point at which every converging instinct tells us that the most natural way of expressing our total longing is in and through the business of prayer.

This intuitive leap, however, is bigger than it sounds, and I spent the following four sessions analysing some of the points in the graph of the trajectory of this leap through which, in retrospect at least, we see ourselves to have passed on the way to the haven we finally discover in prayer: first, the sense of an indwelling presence in the depths of our being graciously and gratuitously bestowed by the living God, so that the leap could in fact be more fittingly described in terms of a descent, or grateful relapse, or collapse into that presence, and its healing silence; secondly, there are the vital hints derived from other human spirits who have preceded us in the tradition, the light of the eyes, the grace of their speech, the style of their lives, and the witness of spiritual literature; thirdly, the ongoing, and growing, awareness of a kind of moral grain, an invitatory call, running through the circumstances of our lives, and always, when followed, seeming to point and lead to the mystery of encounter; and lastly, the faith-provoking experience of observing a Christian Eucharist.

By tracks such as these we finally reach the place of understanding, and thus find ourselves praying. But at once we are surprised to find that the exercise is by no means one-sided. We are in a relationship, a dialogue, which, as in the early stages of a significant human relationship, tends to be obscure, baffling, and not infrequently turbulent.

Nevertheless, as the dust settles, and as some kind of stability supervenes, we may well find ourselves predominantly aware of two great new features marking this relationship: first, a sense of perceiving something we weren't aware of before, but perceiving it in an oddly contradictory fashion, seeing, yet not seeing, 'seeing him who is invisible', what Cuthbert Butler called 'a dim yet direct perception'. In the more elaborate account of Bishop Hedley, as a mid-nineteenth century Roman Catholic Bishop of Newport, to which I expect to return, it is 'a spreading, silent, sense of something near at hand, vague in outline, colourless and dim'.

Secondly, there is a sense of what we slowly recognise as union with what is perceived. So Hedley goes on to say that the 'spreading, silent sense' he talks about is accompanied by ardent love. St John of the Cross similarly speaks of 'a substantial touch' of God in the depths of the soul.

Now it is of the nature of relationships to develop, and this one is no exception. 'Nothing continues in one stay'. Even human relationships appear to have an endless capacity for growth, and the same applies to our relationship with the being of God. Not, of course, in my view at least, that God himself is capable of growth. He is infinitely all he could ever be, and wills to be and do; yet the Christian experience is that no term can be placed to the quality of the friendship to which he chooses to admit us through the economy of grace.

So, taking a large span of, say, thirty years, to cover the critical period of development between the twenties and fifties, the universal experience of growth in this new relationship is always in the direction of simplicity, inwardness, immediacy, and intensity. This can be said absolutely, however much individuals may vary in their rate of growth, or whatever the crises, interludes, diversions or disasters that occur in each one's history.

The first few years are often tempestuously happy, very like the initial stages of being in love, especially for the first time. The rapture of spirit, mind and heart is fierce enough to spill over into a sense of physical well-being. The human soul, seized with the sense of having stumbled at last, after untold travail, on its last end, the very thing it was created for, embraces this final good as lovers do each other, with the vehemence of passion. The whole life is consumed by this holy desire, and every department of it frequently transformed by its light and heat. 'In thy light shall we see light' was one of Augustine's favourite texts.

It is indeed an igniting of all one's powers, and the centering of these on the figure of the Beloved, the living Christ. One begins to understand why that text from the Song of Songs, 'my beloved is mine and I am his', became the driving force of St Bernard's life, and how he in turn made it the driving force of so much of the spirituality of the Middle Ages.

Each life has its supreme hour, when a corresponding effort is made which cannot be repeated. And this initial phase of Christian prayer often proves the occasion of precisely such effort. When the new passion for Christ, his light and sovereign goodness, gradually awakens us to the full extent of our sin and failure and general shabbiness, the result is the onset of a struggle between Christ and evil, between Christ and our own egoism, which rocks life to its depths. One slowly wakes up to the sombre fact, so wonderfully depicted by C.S.Lewis, in *The Great Divorce*, that Christ and sin cannot dwell together in the same heart.

This struggle with our more immediate and obvious sins has given the name of the purgative way to this initial phase. And we might note in passing how natural it is to slip into the habit of identifying Christian life in general with prayer, since it is in the act of prayer more than any other that one becomes intensely aware of one's state before God, and commitment to him; for prayer is the means by which every aspect of Christian life is internalised and made to come alive.

But this purgative phase has a further mark. It is now that the individual life is turned literally inside out by the realisation that, if prayer is really as significant as we are saying it is, then it must become the centre of our existence, not just a polite extra stuck on the circumference, or, to change the metaphor, one of Wittgenstein's loose cogs. Looking back on my own life I can remember no revolution so painful or far-reaching as this. One begins to see that for the time being at least, until one is strong to stand on one's own feet, one's life in this matter must be supported, buttressed, regulated by some sort of rule, which by its very nature will express the primacy of Christ's claim. Sheer clock time has to be given to prayer, and, what is more, the cream of that time.

Here, then, are some of the positive aspects of this early phase of serious prayer. But there is also the negative, shadow, side which can't be overlooked. For instance, this is often a time of intense introspection and preoccupation with our own thoughts and feelings. Like people newly in love, we are highly susceptible to the least changes of mood, rather more in love with love than with the serious business of loving. It will be a long time before we feel the force of that remark of St Francis de Sales, that 'there is a great difference between being occupied with God who gives the contentment, and being busied with the contentment God gives'.

And so it is, as with lovers, there comes a moment when this initial phase of sheer happiness comes to an end, sometimes with startling suddenness. And for a Christian, not to be forewarned can mean dreadful desolation, if not, in some cases, the abandonment of all further effort to pray. It's all been a cheat, we feel. And yet, if one looks again at the analogy of the lovers, one sees it was bound to happen sooner or later. The glory of the flesh has been explored; but this, we realise, is not an end in itself, but, as Berkeley Noel put it,

Mere side reverse of spiritual grace.

Through this glory the personality is now encountered in its strange, frightening depths. A new phase begins: two wills are finally engaged. St John of the Cross uses another analogy; he compares the early happy years to the first kindling of a log in a fire. To begin with all is crackle and flame and brightness, and a sense of progress as the bark is burnt off. If you'll forgive a childhood reminiscence, the business of lighting fires with paper, sticks and coal used to have a deep fascination for me as a boy. Putting match to paper, watching the sticks ignite, and listening to what Wordsworth called 'the flapping of the flame', especially if the morning was frosty, was an absorbing pleasure. But this was always followed by a sense of sadness as the flames died down: and yet one knew it had to come, if the initial brightness was to be transformed into real heat and the larger masses of coal ignited. In the early years the soul is full of bright emotion but not much strength.

St John of the Cross is quite matter-of-fact about all this, and with psychological perceptiveness suggests it is simply the outer crust of our sensuality that God has been penetrating in order to reach the core of our being, the mystery of our self, which is the will. In short, we come to the end of the phase of being in love with love, of what spiritual writers call 'sensible devotion' or 'spiritual sweetness'. With a jolt, a new experience of general drabness brings us down to earth and begins to teach us that what is required is a love deeper than anything we have known hitherto, *love in a new degree*, as T.S.Eliot put it, pure love acting through the will, learning to serve God for his own sake, not for the joy he gives. So what is needed, indeed, all that is possible now, is a very different kind of prayer: a simple clinging with mind and will to the sheer fact, even, sometimes, the mere memory of God; going on from day to day, keeping our ship on course by pure faith in the dark, taught by every instinct that there is in fact no other way.

This is the first great crisis; but there is another, very similar, which in some cases may all occur simultaneously. The sense of mental clarity fades. Merely thinking about God and all He is loses its old exhilaration. It's like leaving the sunlight on a climb, and being slowly enveloped in cold grey mist. The summit is no longer in view: there is nothing to see, and nothing to do but climb, which one does, again by a kind of instinct, simply following the lift of the ground.

What does this mean? We might have expected the demise of spiritual sweetness if we'd thought hard enough; but this kind of loss is different and strange. We can see we needed to be weaned from merely delighting in our feelings about God: it is harder to see we also need weaning from our own thoughts about him. But we do need this, because our pleasure in these thoughts, which can be very keen, is as serious a manifestation of egoism as sensual indulgence in spiritual feeling, and much deeper. And because deeper, it is more serious, even a kind of idolatry, because with such thoughts we are trying to depict God, analyse Him, reduce Him to manageable proportions, get him taped; and we have to be taught that this is forbidden ground. 'To whom will you liken me? saith the Lord'. The theologians tell us we can apprehend God, but not comprehend him. He will not be enclosed in any man's mind. Our neat mental constructs need shattering, as a pot by a plant.

So again, what do we do? Go back to the analogy of climbing. The remedy for the loss of the sweet sense of the sun's warmth is simply to plod on step by step in chilling greyness. The remedy for the loss of the invigorating sense of light and direction is roughly the same. The mere fact of the ground rising beneath our feet tells us that this is the direction we have to take. In both experiences of loss there is a painful sense of being stripped of something we had assumed was ours by natural right: happiness and light. To be deprived of either or both is to be thrown back on the only course left, to seek God deliberately in dryness, perplexity and darkness, through sheer application of the will aided, sometimes without our knowing, by grace. You remember The Cloud of Unknowing defines prayer as 'a naked intent of the heart stretching after God'. Well, here it is: the nakedness is that of the will. Here, too, is Augustine's 'holy desire', seeking God only for Himself in the mystery of his being. If it sounds highfaluting or impossibly rarefied, think once more of the experience of lovers. They have to accept the end of the romantic phase of their love for the greater good of reaching the mystery of each other's personal being. Harder still, they have to forego that habit, which is the ruin of so many marriages, of assuming that the one can know the other absolutely, has got him or her 'taped', and read them like a book, the deepest injury our bourgeois culture teaches us to inflict, in this world of stereotyped reactions of the TV screen. Lovers grow to realise they are in the presence of something that cannot be fathomed in its ultimate depths: that their only hope of entering deeply into it is to give up the attempt, to be content to be known by the other rather than to know, or to receive revelation as the other wills.

So what is the upshot? How do we emerge from this double crisis in our life of prayer? Very much as lovers do: by serving and revering the mystery of the other. By simple perseverance in the act of prayer, the business of prayer, and in the practical obligations of Christian living - for we all have to go on living whatever state we are in - by the constant expression simply of desire, one gradually emerges into a new stage of intuitive awareness of God which becomes the substance, as also the guiding-light of one's life. Slowly the cold and darkness of the 'cloud of unknowing' give way to a new kind of light and a new kind of stillness. And the person concerned is now a changed person, deeply purified in heart and mind and will, no longer measuring everything by the standard of his own comprehension, but content to absorb the new sense of interior light and reality through the action of the Spirit upon him. This state of intuitive awareness, which some writers have called the 'prayer of simplicity', or 'simple regard', is basically one in which all one's fragmentary insights have begun to flow together into a single track of intuitive, comprehensive sight, aided as always by the Spirit of truth himself.

This phase, which characterises the greater part of the lives of many Christians, is, incidentally, also the beginning of contemplation. Until the Reformation this was not regarded as anything extraordinary, but rather as the natural outcome of a life of serious effort in the realm of prayer, an experience in which, as we saw at the beginning, the main ingredients are: a sense of union with God in the heart and will; coupled with a sense of actual, though dim perception of Him in the ground of the soul, a knowledge of which the medium is not cleverness but love. We come back to Bishop Hedley's definition: *a spreading silent sense of something near at hand, vague in outline, colourless and dim, accompanied by ardent love.*

So we press on, always, once again, in the direction of simplicity, inwardness, immediacy and intensity. But there is a third crisis all of us can expect to face in later years, and it is a very strange and testing one. The two previous crises were concerned with the stripping off of what we had assumed was ours by right, the enjoyment of God and a sense of clear ideas about him. This third crisis is deeper in that it seems to involve loss of control of something we consider to be not only our own but the root of our very being, namely our will. In the strangest way, quite without warning, we seem to enter on a phase in which the vital management of our own life begins to be taken out of our hands. What we had thought to do and hoped to do is somehow deeply thwarted. Nothing goes our way. It is almost as if the face of God were turned against us, all greatly intensified by the natural causes of depression in old age. Absurd, you may think; but not if, like me, you have been brought up, as I said, on the doctrine of De Caussade, that the will of God is mediated through the veil of passing circumstances, through the mystery of the present moment.

Anyhow, once again, the thing simply occurs; and the purpose behind it, in my view, is the final weaning of the will from the pleasure and idolatry of its own self-direction, and the painful replacing of this by a quite new kind of passivity: not lassitude, far from it, but a passivity which renders the will totally alert and sensitive to the promptings of Christ in the soul. And the peculiar nature of this last crisis leaves its imprint on the last phase of many Christian lives, a phase which is marked by a quite new sense of being acted upon rather than acting, very like the intuitive sense of being influenced telepathically by each other's will, so characteristic of elderly couples. St John of the Cross pushes his analogy of the burning log to its logical conclusion when he says that in this last phase the heart of the log itself becomes incandescent with the fire on which it is being consumed. The will of God penetrates us totally till we are purged of that egoism which is the root of our sin. And with this, too, comes the uprising of a quite new joy, the joy in God for which we were created.

VIII

Practicalities

Supposing we have decided to give twenty minutes a day to our prayer, how precisely can we expect to spend those minutes?

Following the lines of my third talk, I suggest we begin naturally by entering, or rather, subsiding, into the depths of ourselves, that is, into the uncreated depths which God himself has formed within those depths, simply to rest in the sense of that interior presence we have already thought about so much. Anthony Bloom quotes John Chrysostom as saying, 'Find the door of your heart, you will find it is the door of the Kingdom of God'. So, Bloom continues, 'it is inward we must turn, but in a very special way ... It is not a journey into my *own* inwardness, it is a journey *through* my own self, in order to emerge from the deepest level of self into the place where He is, the point at which God and I meet' (xvii). Here we have to be infinitely careful not to destroy the healing power of these first moments - the most precious we ever spend - by being conscious in a self-conscious way about them. (I am dwelling on them in detail now of course, because trying to understand the business of prayer is what we are about). But in fact, if you will forgive me pressing an analogy which is the best one I know, the experience of these first moments of silence is like nothing so much as the bliss of exchanging a hug, in which speech is all but impossible, because what is transpiring is so swift and complex as to be quite beyond the range of reasoned expression. Speech is a labour and therefore felt to be clumsy. Coleridge put it powerfully in one of his recently discovered notebooks (No XVII, fol.84). Analysing a moment of the human love relationship, he said, *'I fear to speak, I fear to hear you speak, - so deeply do I now enjoy your presence, so totally possess you in myself, myself in you - the very sound would break the union'*. A hug says all there is to be said in a matter of moments. In other words, perhaps the most delicious aspect of this first taste of interior silence is the sense of relief it brings, like a hug on the other level. Kafka once wrote in his diary, 'Receive me into your arms: they are the depths'. A hug, then, means a sudden uninhibited descent into the depths of the other, without the need or use of speech, using only the swift language of love. It means the joy of mutual recognition and acceptance, each recognising the depths of the other as the depths to which they belong and in which alone they can find total healing on the human level. And it means power: feeding on the life of the other for which one was created.

All this and more is involved in the initial descent into the interior silence of prayer: absolute peace, absolute vitamin; the sense of feeding on pure being. And as we are not at prayer in the presence of our spiritual biographer, we can sink into this silence just as and how we wish: sitting, kneeling, reclining, muttering, groaning - for we shall sometimes be in anguish or in speechless rapture and relief.

Anthony Bloom, if I may turn to him again, (School for Prayer 58-9), says 'real silence is something extremely intense, it has density and it is really alive'. And yet, as he hints, there is a catch in it. 'It is essential', he says, 'to be alert and alive, and at the same time still and relaxed, and this is contemplative preparation for contemplative silence; this very difficult balance between the kind of alertness that will allow you with a completely open mind, completely free from prejudice, from expectation, to receive the impact of anything that will come your way, and at the same time this stillness that will allow you to receive the impact without dreaming into it the picture of your own presence that will be destructive of it.'

The fact of the intensity of prayer at this level and this juncture makes me raise a point which may seem a little perverse, but which I feel is worth thinking about: the intimacy as well as intensity of such prayer makes it difficult for me to comprehend how even husband and wife can pray together, not, of course, in the same room, though even that I should find difficult, but as a kind of spiritual unit, in unison perhaps one could say. There seems to be a uniqueness about each human spirit which is absolute, and cannot somehow be shared, because the divine word to one is not the divine word to another. And I mention this here because I sometimes sense a feeling of strain rising to the surface when people tell me, as they sometimes do, that they regularly pray together, as if this were a kind of achievement they would be ashamed of having missed. But 'no man may deliver his brother' - or even his wife, in the sense of being her ditto - 'so that he must let that alone for ever'.

The essence of prayer, then, is to give up ourselves to the attraction of this interior presence for just as long as it remains possible, which means for as long as self-consciousness does not obtrude. As soon as that happens, the spell is broken, the hug is over, speech begins, we draw apart. Nevertheless, the human and divine have touched and fused, however momentarily, and that is what matters. Just how it matters I hope to return to later when we come to consider the fruits of prayer.

Meanwhile, having returned to the strictly conscious level, how *do* we, at least, how *can* we proceed? By following, I suggest, our instinct to do what is most natural, and feeling our way peacefully through what we might call the spectrum of love. The natural thing would thus seem to be to turn to the business of thanksgiving, just friends or lovers, withdrawing from the ecstasy of a hug, find gratitude for the mere fact of each other the main preoccupation. What else can we be but grateful for the fact of God, and for such a God as we know him to be? For the kind of thankfulness I am talking about, look at the first paragraph of the Gloria in Excelsis. For sheer forgetfulness of self those first words are the most magnificently and stringently cleansing that have ever been written. By the same token, the experience of rising from those depths where the essence of the Kingdom is known, is one which produces a mood of thankfulness rather than any other. And it is surely of the first importance that we should sufficiently indulge it, then consciously cultivate it, especially if we find that gratitude is not our natural bent. For gratitude has, unfortunately, come to have a somewhat artificial sound for far too many people, especially those who have been perpetually pressurised as children into saying 'thank-you' under parental or avuncular threats of one kind or another, and as a result tend to grow up rather in the frame of mind of the little girl who wrote: with admirable frankness: 'Dear Auntie, Thank you for my dolly. I liked it but not much'.

Yet in fact gratitude is as near to the heart of Christian existence as breathing is to the life of the physical organism. Nothing so infallibly indicates our awareness of God's presence within, or control of the changing circumstances of our lives. 'With prayer goes gratitude', says Lady Julian splendidly. 'Thanksgiving is a real, interior, knowledge'. To borrow the analogy employed by Vanstone in that remarkable book, *Love's Endeavour, Love's Expense*, divining the heart of God in any single event is very like discovering the name of the sender when receiving a parcel through the post: it transfigures its meaning. In the same way, our gratitude for some incident changes it from a mere neutral occurrence into some kind of gift, or token of God's purpose, almost a secret sign. But of course it works in either direction. Discerning God's hand makes us grateful; but trying to be grateful helps us to discern his hand, and ultimately his purpose. In a pamphlet he wrote some years ago, *On Praying*, Alan Ecclestone made the point that the habit of gratitude is one of the easiest ways back to the contemplative depths from which we have just emerged. He puts it in his own inimitable way:

'Our praying "Thank you", when it is sparked off by a spontaneous moment of gladness has the potentiality of being deepened, and praying at this point means deliberately prolonging, extending, savouring the expression of gratitude so that it doesn't drop away unused and unexplored. To pray is to make the most of our moments of perception. You pause on the thing that has happened, you turn it over and over like a person examining a gift, you set it in the context of past and future, you mentally draw out its possibilities, you give the moment time to reveal what is embedded in it. As you are doing this, you may be saying Thank-you many times with your lips or you may be silently following the path of appreciation. It is the deliberate extension of the moment of gratitude which is important, whatever means you may employ to bring this about.

In other words, 'following the path of appreciation' constantly leads us back to that speechless loving communion by which our spirits live. Or, to put it slightly differently, in a phrase of Mark Gibbard, in his excellent little paperback, *Prayer and Contemplation*, (p.43), 'In prayer and contemplation we say words *around the silence of loving*, like the beams of light playing around the shining spire'.

So it is again by a natural progression that we move from thanksgiving to intercession. When lovers have finished being grateful for each other, they often find themselves asking 'How's so and so?', and thus move into a new area of the spectrum of love. So too in prayer. One can't be thankful for the dealings of

Providence with oneself without soon becoming concerned with his dealings with those for whom one cares. I don't propose to enter at length into the theology of intercession here: simply to stress that it is an inevitable and natural component of our total prayer life. And I would suggest, briefly, that its mechanism somewhat resembles a child's deflection and concentration of the sun's rays through a magnifying glass; only here the effect is not to burn and destroy but to channel and concentrate the rays of divine love through one's own spirit on to the person one is praying for. In this kind of prayer we offer the raw energy of the human heart and will to be fused with the divine wisdom and energy, and used however and whenever needed. And remember, people actually depend for life on such prayer. To find that they return from the grave sometimes when we pray, and die when we forget, is a strange experience. It is no less strange to find them dying when this is the boon we have positively besought the Lord for them. As that wise woman, Abigail, put it to David, our souls are bound together in the bundle of life with the Lord our God and with each other. No man is an island.

But supposing we have exhausted our capacity to sustain this prayer of outgoing concern - and we should remember it really is a *labour* of love, hard work - what we are then faced with is simply ourselves, one's own self, 'a natural nothing and a superadded sin', as Jeremy Taylor put it with devastating accuracy. One is faced with the need for taking account of this self before God. Yet even the confession this necessarily entails need not be the grim affair it is sometimes purported to be. In an odd way, with the instinct of a poet, Charles Péguy struck the right note in his poem 'Abandonment', in which God himself is the speaker, addressing man:

'I am all for making one's examination of conscience every night', says God.

It's a good exercise.

But after all, you mustn't torment yourself with it to the point of losing your sleep.

At that hour, the day is done, and well done. It doesn't have to be done again.

It's all settled.

Those sins for which you are so sorry, my boy, well, it is plain enough,

My friend, you should not have committed them.

At the time you were still free not to commit them.

Now it's over. So go to sleep, you won't do it again tomorrow'.

What then is left? Does the spectrum extend any further? There is, simply, one's own problematic existence, suspended perilously between Being and non-Being. And since we are positively commanded to cherish ourselves as well as our neighbour, we have to accept, with a certain Christian matter-of-factness, the sobering and oddly exalting truth that the sovereign Lord of the universe has placed a value on this existence of ours which we are not at liberty either to deny or belittle. Hence we arrive at that 'kindly permission', to use Barth's lovely phrase, by which Jesus bids us, almost as a test of faith, to make our requests known to the Father of light; and to ask in no mealy-mouthed fashion either, but with the frankness, rigour, insistence and extravagance of a child. (Indeed, we can take this further, and put petition in a very different key. Anthony Bloom, in his School for Prayer, xvii, says 'The day when God is absent, when he is silent - that is the beginning of prayer. Not when we have a lot to say, but when we say to God, "I can't live without you, why are you so cruel, so silent?" This knowledge that we must find or die - *that* makes us break through to the place where we are in the Presence. If we listen to what our hearts know of love and longing and are never afraid of despair, we find that victory is always there on the other side of it'. 'In a way', he says, 'despair is at the centre of things, at the centre of the storm'.) But, if things are more normal with us, there may well be nothing we need beyond what he has already given us. Even so, there are still the hours immediately ahead of us on which blessing needs to be invoked, and all the chores and tasks for which we have to ask. 'Give me Wisdom that sitteth by thy throne'.

Here, by the way, it may be worth noting how petition, which is even sometimes thought of as almost unworthy to be included in Christian prayer, can, like thanksgiving, quite easily lead to bouts of contemplation. You remember how Peter and John, meeting the lame man at the Beautiful Gate of the temple, tell him first to 'look at us': in just such a way, the mere fact of gazing at God in petition can cause one to forget the actual petition and become preoccupied with him, as so often lovers do with each other when they too make requests. There is a rather moving instance of something similar occurring illustrated in a prayer I noted in the new Oxford Book of Prayer, p.119, apparently by 'an unknown Confederate soldier': it is well worth repeating:

I asked for strength that I might achieve;
I was made weak that I might learn humbly to obey.
I asked for health that I might do greater things;
I was given infirmity that I might do better things.
I asked for riches that I might be happy;
I was given poverty that I might be wise.
I asked for power that I might have the praise of men;
I was given weakness that I might feel the need of God.
I asked for all things that I might enjoy life;
I was given life that I might enjoy all things.
I got nothing that I had asked for, but everything that I had hoped for.

**Almost despite myself my unspoken prayers were answered;
I am, among all men, most richly blessed'.**

Here, with a vengeance, is the education of the heart along another avenue of dependence not mentioned in my first two talks.

So we end. We return to the chores or the maelstrom or whatever our business is. But we don't simply return: we do so in the power of the Spirit, as Jesus did from the desert. As Robert Llewellyn has put it in a brief work, *Prayer and Contemplation*, 'the Christian's activity is the overspill of his prayer into daily life'. As Esther de Waal put it in her study of the Rule of Benedict, p.153, 'we pray from the same base as we live'.

IX

Preliminaries

I want now to turn to some of the preliminary aids to prayer, and especially to contemplation, which are available for our use. And first, the practice I confess I have never much used myself nor found congenial, almost certainly to my own loss, namely meditation. This is a form of preparation for prayer, first reduced to a system by the early Jesuits in the sixteenth century: a way of arousing the mind, will and heart to serve God by means of methodical consideration of some biblical passage or theological truth. (I say I have neglected this probably to my own loss in so far as some of the spiritual writers who have fed me most abundantly have been those who practised meditation seriously. Perhaps the reason for my aversion lies far in the past, when I conceived a strong distaste for the rather rigid systematisation of the Jesuit method. I am all for battering the brain; but I rather feel that the place for that is the study, not one's prayers. And I am also one of those who believe, as C.S.Lewis did, that a stiff volume of doctrine can be as richly devotional as any other. The point I think I am trying to make is that there is a point at which the process of ratiocination can actually become counter-productive, leading to mildly mental frenzy instead of devotion).

The details of the various methods need not concern us here. Sufficient to say that the principle behind them is contained in that phrase of the psalm, 'While I was thus musing, the fire kindled' (39.4). While the mind is musing the fire of love is kindled in the heart and will. St Bernard put it powerfully and picturesquely in one of his Sermons on the Song of Songs (41):

'Don't you see that the intellect discharges for the soul functions analogous to those which the neck performs for the body, since it is through the intellect that spiritual food passes into the soul and is conveyed to the digestive organs of the will and the affections.'

In rather more English idiom, Walter Hook, famous as the Vicar of Leeds in the mid-nineteenth century, said, 'I am generally peripatetic in my devotions', explaining that he read the Bible till he sank into a reverie. This, I believe, illustrates another principle of the first importance, namely that the mind, and particularly the English mind, is essentially synthetic in its working, which means that reflections or considerations tend gradually to fuse together into a single track of what I have called 'intuitive sight'. Hook calls it here by a very English name, 'reverie', for which I believe our old word 'brooding' is an authentic equivalent. Meditation, reflection, call it what you will, can easily lead to spells of contemplation. The same is true, as every priest knows, of the thoughtful saying of the Daily Office.

But let me add a caution here. Reverie is not to be confused with day-dreaming. I use it in the sense suggested by the Shorter OED of a 'fit of abstracted musing, 'a brown study', even Chaucer's 'state of delight'. The basic point is that sheer pressure of thought, rather than mere absence of thought, prevents the mind from seizing, following, elucidating any one strand in particular. The power of articulate language is defeated and suspended, and we reach the state of what Sir Thomas Browne called an *'O altitudo'*. Language falls into abeyance, passion supervenes, and as Pope Gregory the Great put it, 'the soul tastes the very thing that it longs for' in a moment of intuitive sight or love.

A different kind of preliminary, and one which I personally have found fruitful over a great many years, is what is generally known as spiritual reading. Here the aim is the same as in meditation: to feed the mind, and by so doing, to arouse the desire of the heart - not, be it said, to get through as many books as possible. The method is a leisurely, i.e. not lazy or inattentive but detached, drawing of the eye along the printed page until the mind becomes conscious of a fullness and agitation which compels it to relinquish the reading and resort to prayer. As with meditation, reverie ensues at one point or another; separate insights fuse into a general, concentrated intuition of God which compels response. Robert Llewellyn compares the labour of the mind to the flapping of its wings by a large bird in an effort to become airborne. This is one use of spiritual reading.

But such reading can become a form of prayer in itself. In his Spiritual Letters, Dom John Chapman compares its mechanism to the kind of thing that goes on in the mind of a man sitting in his club, ostensibly reading the paper but actually listening to the conversation going on beside him. On the surface level his mind is occupied with the printed page in front of him while his real attention is preoccupied with the conversation. So it is in this kind of contemplative browsing: the conscious mind, the source of all our distractions, as we call them, is occupied with the printed word while the heart is preoccupied with God. I know of no more effective safeguard than this against that disintegrating and devastating power which distractions seem to have over what we like to call our minds, especially in times of stress and confusion. St Teresa once said she had never been near her prayers without a book for seventeen years: the mere sense that a book was beside her was enough to keep her mind tranquil and steady.

But reading is not always a means to an end. Sometimes the book itself is rich and golden, such pure distilled truth, that the mere reading of it is rapture, indistinguishable from worship. Such books, apart from the Bible itself, are not common: it would probably be bad for us if they were; but they come one's way in the providence of God - which, remember, is so meticulous as to reach down to the very books we read, and even the moment when we stumble across them - and then one has the experience Samuel promised Saul of being 'changed into another man'; so that such reading can be used either as a preliminary to prayer, or as a supplement to prayer when the impetus fails, or as prayer itself. I recommend it. In *The Love of Learning and the Desire of God,* itself a golden book, the great Benedictine Jean Leclerq provides a masterly account of this type of exercise, known to the Middle Ages as *lectio divina.* He begins by reminding us (pp.89-90) that:

'In the Middle Ages the reader usually pronounced the words with his lips, at least in a low tone, and consequently he hears the sentence seen by the eyes ... This results in a muscular memory of the words pronounced and an aural memory of the words heard. The meditation consists in applying oneself with attention to this exercise in total memorization; it is therefore inseparable from the *lectio*. It is what inscribes, so to speak, the sacred text in the body and in the soul.'

This repeated mastication of the divine words is sometimes described by the use of the theme of spiritual nutrition. In this case the vocabulary is borrowed from eating, from digestion, and from the particular form of digestion belonging to ruminants. All this activity is, necessarily, a prayer; the *lectio divina* is a prayerful reading. Thus, the Cistercian, Arnoul of Boheriss (in his Speculum Monachorum, written about the year 1200) will give this advice: 'When he reads let him seek for savour not science. The Holy Scripture is the well of Jacob from which the waters are drawn which will later be poured out in prayer. Thus there will be no need to go to the oratory to begin to pray; but in reading itself, means will be found for prayer and contemplation'.

That testimony comes from France. Powerful corroboration comes from a very famous English book, the *Ancrene Riwle* or Guide of Anchoresses, whose anonymous author evidently knew the Cistercian tradition well. He tells them that: 'the remedy for sloth is spiritual joy and the comfort of joyful hope, which comes from reading, from holy meditation, or from the sayings of others. Often, dear Sisters, you ought to say fewer fixed prayers so that you may do more reading. Reading is good prayer. Reading teaches us how to pray and what to pray for, and then prayer achieves it. In the course of reading, when the heart is pleased, there arises a spirit of devotion which is worth many prayers' (p.127). What more can one add, except that remark of Jerome, 'let your book support your drooping head'.

So much, then, for reading. I want now to turn to another crucial area, in which each must work out, by experimenting over the years, their own pattern of practice: I mean the relation of private to liturgical, and especially Eucharistic prayer. There must be balance here, otherwise strange things inevitably occur.

It is probably true to say that each of us tends to be either an institutionalist or individualist in this matter: so addicted to the system, so carried away by public worship, that it rarely occurs to us to reflect or pray in private; or else, so introverted, so preoccupied by temperament with our own interior and spiritual life, that public worship presents itself almost as a distraction, even as a somewhat painful duty. You may know the story of the Englishman, travelling in Bulgaria, I think it was, who, rather to his embarrassment, found himself sharing a bedroom with an orthodox monk. Kneeling conscientiously by his bed to say his prayers before retiring, he was baffled and astonished to see the monk get straight into bed without the slightest attempt to pray.

The Englishman knew hardly any religion but that of private prayer; the monk could hardly conceive of prayer apart from the company of his brother monks. Thus, it is possible so to rely on the current of public worship to carry us along that we almost cease to have a soul of our own; on the other hand, to be so concerned with our own interior life that we quite lose sight of the fact that it is a *common* salvation to which we are heirs.

But there is something of a bias in one direction or the other in almost every parish as well as in nearly every soul, and hard work it is to maintain the health and balance of the Body of Christ when its members are made of such mysterious stuff. Yet the balance must be held, for in fact there is no fundamental incompatibility between the two. This doesn't come easily however, to the mind of the average, rather individualist, Englishman. It is hard for him to realise that the Gospel is good news of a 'common salvation'; not given to satisfy a private interest of his own in God, but to build up a corporate body, brought into being by the sole power and action of Christ.

His Body, the Church, reached its high point of self-awareness as his creation at the supreme moments of the Last Supper and Pentecost, and it has maintained that awareness ever since by the celebration of that Supper, its re-enactment, it's re-presentation. All Christ was and did for us is rehearsed and renewed in mind and heart with each celebration. Each disciple becomes fully himself only in fellowship with the Body, just as personality needs the matrix of the family in which to grow. Nevertheless, as the members of a family cannot use their togetherness to shelter from the task and pain of developing minds of their own, so each individual Christian is committed to search out and evaluate for themselves all that it means to be incorporated in Christ. You remember Berkeley Noel: *'Each is himself by universal grace'*.

Now, as you know, I have already devoted the whole of our sixth session to the matter of the Eucharist. But my interest then was in the Eucharist as a means of awakening faith. Here, the interest is different. Faith is already assumed. Here, the concern is that the truth of the Gospel, which is ultimately and initially a corporate possession, should be personally appropriated by prayer in the heart of the believer. By the same token, his awareness of the depth of his (or her) own being, as recreated in Christ, is a vital contribution to the corporate awareness of Christ's presence in the Eucharistic action. Indeed, the fact that there is sometimes a sense of utter flatness and deadness at the Sunday Eucharist may well be due, as much as anything, to the shallow perfunctoriness of the lives we are leading individually during the week. So what are the implications? Each has to work them out for himself in terms of his own life. For myself, I can only testify to the nourishing effect of a peculiarly Anglican four-course menu starting with Matins, proceeding with the Eucharist, followed by a period of spiritual reading, and concluded with private prayer.

But of course it would be absurd to expect this of the person who has to catch the 7.30, though, oddly enough, it is not impossible for the person who need not be in the office till 9.0, provided they start early; and even the man who has to be on the shop floor at 8.0 can still manage to say Matins and share the Eucharist on one weekday a week, and that is much. (This is something we shall have to discuss very carefully afterwards, since my particular outlook and presuppositions are hopelessly distorted by the life I am committed to lead.) Obviously, the full menu I have just outlined is generally speaking mainly a priest's fare, though, astonishingly, there is nothing in it exclusive to priests. But at least what these four items do provide is a fully balanced diet: first, the iron ration of the Daily Office, the nuggetty truth of the Gospel, severe yet bracing, marvellously prepared for digestion on each several day of the year, the church's marching orders for the day, you might say; next all that truth warmed and made alive at the altar by participation in the Passion of Christ; then reflection on it in a spell of contemplative reading; and finally, a time in which to digest it all, especially the food of the Eucharist, in the profundities of prayer. It sounds heavy fare; but in fact to go straight from it, from the Office, from the altar, from prayer, to the strains of the office, the other office, with a small 'o', or the cataract of the day's traffic, is to go mysteriously strengthened and refreshed. We stride out of the porch in the power of the Spirit as Jesus did from the desert into Galilee. This is the real overspill of prayer into daily life, which is harder to experience if we are only in church on Sundays. To begin with the shock is severe, but infinitely slowly the transition becomes natural, and naturalness is what we began with. As Thomas à Kempis put it, *'in the morning fix thy good purpose, and in the evening examine thy ways.'*

X

Rules

We spent our last session considering various preliminaries to prayer, getting prayer airborne, so to speak. I want now to think about the matter of rules, considered simply as supports for the practice of prayer as such, quite apart from any particular techniques.

This is an aspect of the life of prayer which may not greatly appeal to many, and may positively repel some. But the question for us is, simply, can we sustain a life of serious prayer without them? If we can, well and good; if not, should we not at least consider their role? Speaking for myself, I only know that but for the help of rules, my own life would have continued in the chaos in which the claim of Christ found it in my early twenties.

But before we go further perhaps we ought to revert to fundamentals to remind ourselves of the purpose of our whole exercise. We are concerned with Christianity as the recreation of men and women in the lost likeness of Christ, beginning with the restoration of our nature to its original image through an incarnate life of unbroken obedience, and the subsequent diffusion of Christ's immolated life through his mystical Body. However crude this is as a picture of the Christian schema, I believe it is sufficient to indicate that our main concern as bearers of the Christian name is the reproduction of Christ's obedience in the context of our own lives.

But this is in fact a huge revolution, totally dislocating to the fixity and ferocity of our self-will, that egoism which constitutes the root of our sin. Only a few days before putting these remarks together I happened to see, as you may have done, the last instalment of a TV series called "Making Waves". The instalment ended with a piece of obscenity exceeding anything I personally have witnessed, even on TV, and which you might well call the absolute quintessence of modern paganism: it was a reverential view of a private luxury cruiser, sitting like a golden idol, high and lifted up on its stocks for our worship, and costing a sum total of £5 million. We were conducted briefly, and again reverentially, round the interior, all of superlative quality; but I noticed there was no chapel. For a sea-going boat, with every modern convenience, you might have thought there might have been just a tiny oratory, but there was no such thing. The boat was the perfect monument to the principle of pleasing yourself.

Now the essence of pleasing oneself is using your time precisely as you yourself wish, with no let or hindrance whatever. The essence of the Christian life, on its practical side, is the offering, the consecration, of all time to God as the framework within which his will is to be done. Prayer is the vital link between Christ's life of obedience and ours, his sonship and ours, his mind and ours; the establishment of the revolution effected once for all in the days of his flesh and its reproduction in the days and circumstances of our flesh. And my point this evening is that the agony of such a transition may be at least eased, though perhaps no more, by the expedient of simple rules to aid the mind and the heart and the will to face the ongoing, and apparently illimitable consequences of embracing the mind that was in Christ Jesus.

That remarkable spiritual guide, Dom John Chapman, says in one of his letters that communion with God is conditioned by time spent in prayer, and by solitude. Time is our most precious commodity, and the use we make of it infallibly indicates our ultimate concerns and priorities. To have a rule about prayer may therefore be the only way in which we can harness its power for the re-ordering of our lives.

The first of these rules is to pray every day. Christians find that a day without prayer is a day strangely lost, even a dangerous thing, what the old Romans called a *dies non*, the kind of day Job prayed should not appear in the calendar of the months. There is something almost frightening about the folly and hubris of embarking on a day without it, as foolish as a mariner neglecting his compass for a day. The days of our life are linked together by prayer as the miles of phone wires are linked by poles. Destroy one pole and you disrupt the whole line. But given the habit of regular prayer, one's life becomes a connected whole, growing continually in the knowledge of what it is to exist as a man in the image of God, created to know the ultimate reality of the righteousness of God in Christ. 'It is when we are upon our knees', said William Law, 'that we are upon the utmost heights of human greatness'.

But it is precisely in the dailiness of prayer that the essence of the conflict resides. And if you want confirmation of this, go back to what I was saying in our 7th session about the recognised crises in the development of normal prayer, especially the onset of the period of inner moral purgation after the initial phase of spiritual or sensible devotion has passed. There come times - again let me remind you of their modern portrayal in C.S.Lewis's Great Divorce when Christ is in naked conflict with the roots of evil in us, when the crux is not so much whether we shall or shall not give way to a particular temptation, but whether we will or will not put ourselves at his disposal again in an act of prayer: there are so many options so immediately more attractive.

And here you see the meaning of a second possible basic rule for easing prayer into the normal structure of our lives: to pray at the same time every day, at least where this is a physical possibility. This is where rules really bite. It is something immeasurably important to give the cream of the day to God; it is hardly less important to put aside time for him before the pleasure or the business of the evening begins. (Perhaps you think prayer twice a day excessive. But then, just as a day in politics is a very big thing, so is a day in the life of any Christian. Anything can happen in a day; and it is often the thought of going to our prayers in the evening that makes a decisive difference to what we do or don't do in those deserts of time which sometimes occur somewhere about the middle of a day). By this means the day is turned inside out. Instead of being filled entirely with our own obsessive concerns, ending before sleep with an attempt to pray entirely vitiated by weariness, its whole course is turned into an orbit consciously and regularly revolving around two ellipses, our morning and evening prayer.

But this same rule has a further, hidden, advantage. There is of course no particular virtue in praying at one hour rather than another. On the other hand, to wrench the day into subservience to Christ by keeping to the hour of prayer at whatever cost to natural inclination is no small matter. Indeed, in my own experience there is nothing that so clearly asserts the authority of Christ over daily life and one's own wayward will. Such a rule has the effect of strengthening the will as well as simplifying life and delivering it from the excessive, strangulating clutter of rival concerns. A housewife keeps her kitchen utensils on hooks and in drawers around her, so that she only has to put out her hand to take what she wants. She knows 'where things go'. By the same token, it is a good thing to know where things fit on the face of the clock; and if this is our rule, then the mere approach of the hour for prayer on the clock face is sufficient to settle all manner of debates with oneself. We don't ask, what shall I do now? We go and pray.

And this has unexpected consequences. An undergraduate once asked me, with some concern, whether such a rule of prayer didn't dislocate the day. The strange truth is that it actually stretches the day to its maximum extent and capacity, as poles do a marquee, so that instead of being able to do less, as we fear, we find ourselves accomplishing more. In addition, the rule, or rather the experience of God in prayer which the rule facilitates, gradually establishes a whole new sense of priorities in the heart, so that as the years go by many of the things we had thought essential drop away as useless

Here we stumble on something very secret and very near the heart of ordinary Christian understanding: the gradual realisation of the attraction of Christ's staggering simplicity and the rationality in which it is grounded. Here we return to the doctrine I think I at least hinted at in our first or second session: the great doctrine of Christian Humanism, the idea that we are only fully humanised as we are fully Christianised. But this is an idea we stumble on slowly, and embrace even more slowly, because every instinct of commercialism is geared to persuading us it is nonsense, that the last thing we need is Christ, and that the first thing we need is the indulgence of every want, whim, pleasure, or whatever.

But remember that the cultivation of simplicity, which seems to be one of the essentials of the Christian life the world over, and down all the ages, is not to be considered as an end in itself, as a new fad on a par with The Good Life, or the Getting-away-from-it-all mania. Simplicity is a pre-condition of power, just as a healthy body is the pre-condition of efficiency in the conduct of life generally. Only when our lives are stripped and simplified from the suffocating clutter of ungoverned self-indulgence are we free not only to demonstrate the sanity of Christ but have room to put ourselves out, 'displease ourselves', as the New Testament puts it, for the love of others.

So, a rule of prayer doesn't entail a special habitat, in the country, or far off in the Hebrides. It can be implemented in the homeliest suburb or slum. And here we come in sight of a third possible rule: that of praying, if feasible, in the same place every day; and what better place than the one actually built exclusively for the purpose, the house of prayer, however dingy or worthy of Pevsner's contempt, like the little chapelry in Reach, my second parish, which he said is so ugly it 'must be seen to be believed'. But even such places become dear and transformed when consecrated to prayer over the years. They can even become the bridgehead of a ministry, not to say a focal point of worship for a community in a quite new way, a trysting place where God is known, or at least known to be knowable. And there is a fourth rule we might consider: to pray for the same length of time each day. Here again, mysteries are concealed beneath simplicities. The heart is deceitful and can suggest the most powerful reasons for curtailing the period of prayer on any occasion, usually on those days when we need it most. Robert Llewellyn quotes Colin Morris as saying, 'we are not likely to pray everywhere all the time unless we learn to pray somewhere some of the time'. A rule about time not only keeps us to our prayer, but in doing so reveals the heart's treachery, and thus confirms us in self-knowledge. Very often, too, in the minutiae of God's providential dealings, we receive some intimate secret blessing we should have missed had we left our prayers when flesh and self-will prompted.

Lastly, I would remind you of one sovereign rule formulated by Dom John Chapman: 'pray as you can and not as you can't, and pray much'. In other words, whatever our method, which must suit our temperament, if we give ourselves generously the Spirit of God himself teaches us how best to pray, and draws us into the mysteries only revealed in prayer.

Finally, then, just a word about the fruits of prayer, which I want to discuss at rather more length in our next session. We return, first, to Coleridge's dictum, that prayer is the means by which belief is transformed into action. St Augustine once observed that 'Peace is the tranquillity of order'. And it is supremely the tranquillity of the order of the heavenly city experienced in prayer which slowly comes to be reflected in the tenor of our lives. Tranquillity nowadays has some rather negative overtones, suggesting perhaps quiescence or the mere absence of commotion. But what it really describes is the quality so characteristic of Jesus, the huge, inexhaustible reserves of peace and rationality deriving from those times, often of amazing length - which he spent in prayer; the power, which never failed him, of directing thought and action into obedience to the love and wisdom of the Father's will.

And with this vital interplay between prayer and activity, so strikingly manifest in Jesus, we come full circle to our starting point, that of prayer as the supremely natural thing for the Christian, even though, paradoxically, supernaturally prompted and maintained. If the rhythm of prayer and action, each both feeding and creating the demand for the other, doesn't feel as natural as breathing in and out, as urgent and compelling as the exchanges of lovers, then something is deeply wrong and will lead sooner or later to strain and even collapse in some area of life. The finest description I know of that necessary interaction comes from the Flemish mystic, John Ruysbroeck, in *The Adornment of the Spiritual Marriage* (64.5), where he says:

'God demands of us both action and fruition in such a way that one never impedes, but always strengthens the other. And therefore the

most inward man lives his life in these two ways: namely in work and rest. And in each he is whole and undivided; for he is wholly in God because he rests in fruition and he is wholly in God because he loves in activity'.

XI

Christian Initiative - fruit of prayer

I promised in this last session to try to say something about the fruits of prayer, since, if prayer has even a fraction of the significance we say it has, such fruits must be unmistakable, even momentous. Momentous indeed, is probably the literal truth, if we adopt the secondary meaning of 'momentum' as 'weight'. Augustine said 'love is the soul's weight' (De Mus. 6.29); *'amor meus pondus meum'* - 'my weight is my love' (which should be a comfort to weight-watchers). The soul's force, therefore, considered either as weight or movement, is generated in its prayer, where it consorts with reality and takes on its qualities. What those qualities are we have been noticing intermittently as we have made our way, so we don't need to explore them in detail now: sufficient to repeat that all growth in prayer is growth in the simplicity which is born of relentless engagement with truth, but expressing itself increasingly in obedience, zest, order, mildness, wisdom and charity, easy enough to enumerate, but the business of all eternity, one imagines, to explore and appropriate fully. [I had it in mind to attempt to discuss something rather different, though in the event I may succeed in doing no more than sparking off a discussion].

My main point can be put in a sentence: if prayer is what we are claiming it is, concerned with bringing the spirit to a dim yet direct perception of God, and a sense of union with him in the depths of its being, should not this generate in Christians an original initiative sufficient to renew the Church, if not the earth? If prayer is the means by which the risen Christ himself comes to live in the heart, shouldn't we be looking for signs of 'the world being turned upside down', as it was by Paul and his companions? If our circumstances do really have a direction and are not random; if they are charged with a mysterious, living, inviting presence and promise, to which our minds are gradually awakened, accustomed and sensitized by prayer, then the potential here for Christian initiative is strictly incalculable. The God who acts on the souls of awakened Christians - not forgetting the consciences of that multitude of admirable people who cannot yet accept the Christian Gospel - this God is the one who is slowly guiding history towards his own goals, one of which, perhaps the highest, as William Temple taught us to see, is our 'full development in a community of free persons' under the liberating sovereignty of his love. You can see, then, how the life work of many Christians who have changed the course of history has arisen: it has suggested itself to their minds through their being led on from day to day to follow Christ in new paths through this double habit of prayer and the sense of him continually and urgently present. It is the risen Christ, after all, who says 'Behold, I make all things new'.

So what I am suggesting to you now, if you can bear the vagueness and thinness, and perhaps, you may think, the sheer impossibility of it, is that you ought to be prepared to find yourself being called to follow Christ along strange new paths for the sake of his Gospel. Let me remind you of that promise of 'the new name written on the white stone', the new identity bestowed on the person who endures, sticks it out, the identity which, as I said, is a kind of inalienable secret between Christ and each soul, the name no one knows save he or she who receives it.

Don't think I'm suggesting you all go off and think up a new gimmick. The time for that, I think, has passed. What we now have to face and carefully attend to, is that not only is the tide of religion fast running out (of this country at any rate), but paganism, not simply mindless secularism, is now very much on the offensive - witness James Burke and René Cutforth - so that more and more it becomes incumbent on Christians to have a care for the style of life they adopt which, in St Peter's terms, means having clear reasons to offer not only for their beliefs, but for what they do and don't do, and the way they do it. T.R.Glover once said 'the friends of Jesus had got his mind and knew what to do' (*Jesus in the Experience of Men*, 1921, p.194). In another small book, *The World of the New Testament*, p.165, which he wrote ten years later, in 1931, he says, 'Plato concerns himself mainly with safeguards, Jesus wholly with venture'. One is almost tempted by remarks such as this to suggest that Christians should actually be aiming at a new culture; but I think any such culture would soon be dated and exhausted. Glover indicates a sounder way when he quotes Harnack's phrase, 'infinite love in ordinary intercourse' as the secret of the Gospel's spread (*Jesus in the Experience of Men*, p.193). But we should not forget a remark he makes in a third small book, *Christ in the Ancient World*, p.10, 1929: 'Christianity triumphed because it squared best with the world's best intelligence'. To which I feel constrained to add a longer passage from p.56: 'The Fourth Gospel records Jesus as saying "I came that they might have vitality, and overflow with it"; and they did. They really believed what they said; they really had made new experiments in living and had had experience of new facts and new factors, and they were happy. They made little pretence to culture at first; Paul avowed to the Corinthians that he had none in their sense of it. Plato had once spoken of dealers in ideas, retailing them with the shopkeeper's praise of his wares; and Paul, no doubt by accident, uses the same word - he will use no tradesman's art in puffing or booming the Gospel, but talk facts, set down the thing as it was, conscious that he is in the sight of God. Christian preaching and teaching are to be as sincere as the sunlight. Experience, happiness and sincerity go a long way to create literature'.

So what are the options? This is the crux of the problem. Christians are sometimes so deeply oppressed with the sense of their own insignificance and impotence that they do get betrayed into embracing notice-catching gimmicks sometimes; but Anthony Harvey has taught us in his recent Bampton Lectures, *Jesus and the Constraints of History*, to see that Jesus could only have made the impact he did by operating stringently within the limits of the culture and thought-forms of his day. We live in a perverse age, which pinches the mind at many points; but it is the present age and no other we are called to serve and win. We therefore have to accept John Robinson's view that Christians of all ages are called to act on the culture of their time by following the action of salt, not standing gleaming white and useless in the cellar, but impregnating and seasoning in the act of disappearing. We are faced first, then, with the daunting but exhilarating fact, which was not quite an established fact even when I was ordained, that Christians now have no privileges in England, as they most certainly hadn't under the Roman Empire till the conversion of Constantine early in the fourth century. All influence therefore derives solely from the inherent quality of what we have to offer; so we have to look, though necessarily in a cursory fashion, at what it is we do have to offer.

Springing immediately to mind, though I am not competent to assess its relative significance - is the quality of our common life in the church. Westcott always insisted that this was the principle weapon in the conversion of the Empire, more important than her organisation, more important even than her spiritual and philosophical writings, because, as Alec Vidler used to say, that common life demonstrated a unique capacity to transcend the divisions of the ancient world between slave and free, rich and poor, men and women, Greek and barbarian, Roman citizen and colonial, or, as we should say, white-collar and blue-collar, super-tax and social security, public school and comprehensive, classical and pop, Liberal, Labour and Conservative. As Vidler put it, 'no such all-inclusive society had ever been seen'. This is still one of the joys of life in the English church, though of course that church is always having to take itself to task when it finds its individual congregations are lapsing from the dignity of being the holy common folk of God, the *sancta plebs Dei*, into a clique. It is still wonderful for an Anglican parish priest to feel he can at least knock on any door he likes, and indeed traverse the entire social scale in the course of an afternoon. Take this out of many communities, and little is left but contiguous, barely gelling, non-interacting groups. In the Church, as it has been said, 'we can be of the same mind even when not of the same opinion'.

But if we leave this general area of the common life of the Church, we are inevitably committed to looking at the way Christians can dedicate themselves to God in the public and social life of the country to which they belong, and their contribution here can never count for nothing. Alasdair Macintyre, in his remarkable book, *After Virtue*, (1981), says, p. 29, 'characters in general ... are those social roles, which provide a culture with its moral definitions'. So, he says, (26-7), 'the culture of Victorian England was partially defined by the characters of the Public School Headmaster, the Explorer and the Engineers and that of Wilhelmine Germany was similarly defined by such characters as those of the Prussian Officer, the Professor, and the Social Democrat'. How is it defined to day? I am no Alistair Cooke, but I think he would assent to the view that over and above competence, which is a *sine qua non* of effectiveness to-day, he would require a certain element of integrity which places the demands of truth above all other.

And here, in my innocence, I think I want to stick my neck out and say we still owe a lot to intelligent Christians in politics, who likewise value truth above all things. Walter James a few years ago wrote a fine book on The Christian in Politics, which derives much of its power from being not a blue-print of utopia, but a largely factual description of the ways things were then (1962), and I believe still are. No politician to-day cuts ice by explaining that he is a Christian: only, being a Christian, by speaking as faithfully to the point as his training in religion and politics demands. This is one of the elements in political life which makes memoirs so fascinating.

But I think there may be more to it than integrity, much though that is. Glover, in *Christ in the Ancient World*, 78, has an illuminating passage on the decline of that world. 'The thing that above all ruined society', he says, 'was the increasing withdrawal of responsibility from the individual. With the fall of democracy, citizenship with its duties and its training went. Of course there were trifling things to do, which could be entrusted to impotent little local town councils, to bailies and bumbles. Plutarch held magistracies of this kind. But ancient history teaches us that men are made great by great responsibilities. Caesar and the great soldiers and administrators of the Republic were made by having to manage great provinces and great armies, by huge responsibilities. The decline of character in the Empire, conversely, was brought about inevitably by the government seeing to it that ordinary people had nothing to do outside the market. The Christian religion changed all that, till the Church borrowed the names and the plans of the civil administration, bishops and dioceses and so forth. Responsibility, a free initiative, the sense of the future, these are the things that make character; and they were of the very fabric of the Christian life'.

So, in the more limited sphere of local government. Here, in my experience, it is actually possible to see integrity, responsibility, a free initiative, and a hope of the future arising, in a very costly way, directly from the deep springs of religion. And more than these things, too: the sheer will to go on in that brutally unkind world. Merely battling on, however, is not enough. There has to be that reaching out and down to the specific individuals whose statistics make up the problems, and where the qualities of concern and compassion are most fully granted their Christian scope.

Still roughly within the sphere of local government, one might say a word about the Welfare Services. It used to be my lot to look after a small theological college, not a few of whose students had come from that world. So very often vocation to priesthood had been received through the realisation that pedalling the benefits offered by the statutory services stopped short just where real help was needed, in the heart and in the soul and in the mind, but precisely where the social worker's brief did not run. Hence their compelling sense of need to give themselves totally to a pastoral and deeply personal ministry. This I understand and respect. Nevertheless, my respect also goes out very fully to those who remain within the statutory services in order to make them work as well as they can be made to work; and we are all wise enough here to understand what latitude there is between the statutory minimum and the extra mile that even a social worker may go for Christ's sake without exceeding their brief.

That latitude is even wider, perhaps, in the case of the teacher, for whom my respect deepens with every year. There is nothing sadder than the bored and disillusioned teacher. Equally, there are few experiences more heartening than regular contact with teachers who, having passed beyond the years of early natural enthusiasm, are still, for Christ's sake, giving their all year in year out, and who, by the quality of life they impart, and the aptness of their *obiter dicta*, are fulfilling Christ's mission of enabling growing minds to know what it means to be tasting life, and tasting it more vitally.

Perhaps I may insert here still another passage from Glover's book on Christ in the Ancient World, (59): 'the Christian was brought in Christ into a new region of experience. Once that befalls a man of any insight, he stands for ever for exploration of the great things of God; he sets truth before tradition; he has a new feeling for the real and a new happiness in it. He may, by old loyalties, be misguided as to the form in which he expressed his new life; he will have of course all sorts of human limitations; but life is real and serious, and art is real and serious, and they meet whenever they can. It took centuries to reveal what Christ meant in thought and art and literature, giving new value to man, new wonder to God, and a new zest for life in the new intimacy with both, and the call of the Gospel is still to *read what is yet unread in the manuscripts of God*'.

So this, perhaps, is the point where it is right to look at our personal contribution to society as Christians. There is a deep and dark suspicion prevalent in this country that the church is against life: witness, once again, the recent TV series by James Burke, not to mention René Cutforth's remark, made with vigour and relief, 'we've got rid of God, sin, and the Devil'. Glover, in that same book just quoted, can be equally stern in his criticism of Christians. 'Christians', he says 'think terribly slowly at times, they miss the issue, they fight at the wrong angle, emphasise what does not matter and only half realise what counts. All this is true, and it was true in the ancient world. Then, as now, Christians had to share contemporary culture or have none; they deferred then, as now, to contemporary opinion, and were far too trustful of traditional beliefs and accepted results'. But Jesus, you remember, could sum up his entire mission, according to St John, by saying, absolutely without qualification, 'I came that they might have life, and have it more abundantly', or, as Glover translates it, 'have vitality, and overflow with it'. To be in Christ, Paul says, is to be a new creation, a new departure. Such fullness of life, therefore, must be one of the hallmarks of Christian living in any age.

But of course such living will always be subconsciously taking into account the drift of the age in which people find themselves. In a sense they must function much as Walter Hook was described as doing over a century ago at Leeds, 'breasting his bow against the stress like a ship at anchor'; in an age of luxury stressing simplicity; in an age of Puritanism, the goodness of life and creation, in an age of popular movements and slogans, independence of judgement; in an age of sheer materialism, the realm of the inner life.

In other words, we are deeply concerned not so much with what we have to say for ourselves as with our stance, our style of life. In 1975 a laicised Roman priest by the name of Anton Grabner-Haider published a collection of *Letters to a Young Priest*, and perhaps I may, in conclusion, draw on these to illustrate my meaning. Speaking of prayer as 'the totality of linguistic acts of faith' (30), he says, first, 'take your bearings from Jesus' security in God' (31). 'Above all' - and I think this is true of all of us - 'you will be a frontier man, a sign of what lies beyond' (33). Thus, he emphasises Wittgenstein's discovery that language is closely related to a *life-form*, so that, as supremely in the case of Jesus, the speech, the illustrative language, as it were, arises directly from the life-form, not vice-versa. Remember he is talking to a priest, and therefore his reference is limited; but his insights are not limited to priesthood.

Thus, he says, 'the priest is a sign of transcendence, a living sign of God', as indeed any neighbour may suddenly become. Coming down to details, he enumerates some of the specific signs: 'a detached attitude towards possessions; the renunciation of success and achievement; actual service, love and assistance, and occasionally the giving up of one's rights, of one's own wishes'. Such a way of life inevitably, if lived with Christ's own fullness, brings one into conflict with contemporary society. And this prompts Raider to offer some interesting comment on the criticism of contemporary society our life-style must inevitably entail. 'Criticism', he says (56), 'is primarily a life-form. The critic's own life must be a convincing advertisement of his cause'. But criticism of this kind is what he calls *lived*, not simply verbal criticism, and the former must always take precedence over the latter. 'Lived criticism is a living dialogue' (57). 'One needs', he adds, 'to be very careful with criticism and with the spoken word generally. As soon as the words have left your lips you have no more control over them; they do what they please'. Even so, he says, 'never refuse to engage in dialogue' (61). But 'in all this', he cautions. 'my wish is that you may possess that calmness which befits a minister of the Gospel and which we, in our time, did not possess'.

May I return then to Glover just once more. Talking about the life of Athens at the height of her greatness in the age of Pericles in the 5th century B.C., he says *'there is a unity in the age and the people, an integrity (as it has been called) about the citizens; they are whole men, and not decimals'*. It is precisely Christ's call to us to be whole in his likeness.

XII

Afterthoughts

Intercession

Wishes were expressed last week that something should be said in conclusion about two problems: intercession, and the place of the body. So first, intercession.

In order to ground intercession in basic theological truth, we have to go right back to the New Testament and examine the place of the Spirit, i.e., the Holy Spirit, in the whole Christian scheme. If you take a general view, then you can, indeed you must, reach the conclusion that the Spirit is what might be called the 'principle of return' in the created order, i.e., he is ultimately the means by which every corner and level of creation is eventually brought back to its centre and sanity in God, through Christ.

But it must be remembered that this is no quiet philosophical principle we can normally forget about for all practical purposes. The Spirit's action, on the contrary, is a seething fire, with a force of a nuclear wind, 'interceding with sighs too deep for word', in Paul's phrase. Moreover, his action is not external to us, something between himself and the Father, so to speak: his intercession ascends via our very own spirits: he groans within us. How do we know this? There is no way of knowing but plumbing the depths of Christian existence. To meet a human spirit which has lost its bearings is to know a nameless pain. The heart goes out, goes out, moreover, to the heart of the Godhead, which in turn is always reaching out for created spirits and loving them into life. A pale image of the Spirit's force is the ferocity of women when their compassion is aroused by the ill-treatment of children. This is one strand in the complex process we call intercession.

The work of the Spirit is the re-recreation of human spirits in the lost likeness of Christ, the image of God; but, as I say, it is a work profoundly internal, not external, to us who have received its first-fruits.

But we can extend this thread of thought to see it powerfully exemplified in the Gospel story itself. On one occasion, you remember, men bring a paralytic to Christ, and to get to him, actually presume to rip up a man's roof in order to place the man where Jesus simply can't ignore him. This is faith: intercessory faith, if you like; intercession acted out, drawing forth the compassion of Christ. And of course there are parallels: the man they brought who was deaf, and had an impediment in his speech, and besought him to lay his hand upon him, which Jesus promptly did, for he did all things promptly, and in the most painstaking manner. And there was the centurion whose faith on behalf of his servant drew such unparalleled admiration from Jesus. But perhaps most moving of all is the intercession of the ruler of the synagogue on behalf of his daughter. Jesus, instantly responding, is interrupted by the woman troubled by the issue of blood. By the time that is dealt with, the girl is dead, and messages reach the ruler deprecating further action. But Jesus forestalls them with his sovereign word: 'have no fear: only believe', and the girl is raised.

Here is need meeting power; power meeting need, distress confronting love, not for itself, or its own benefit, but for that of others, so that the law of the exchanges of charity on which our world is built comes instantly into operation.

But, as already suggested, in an earlier session, there is still another angle from which to approach this problem. When our human spirit holds up the needs of another spirit before God, it is as if the rays of divine love are deflected and concentrated through the soul of the intercessor on to the soul of the interceded for, and life-giving effects result. Ask for proof, and again one must resort to experience. Souls do return from the brink, or sin, or lostness, when presented before God.

But remember lastly, there is the practical side of intercession, implementing prayer with costly action. The four men who carried the paralytic to Jesus were probably in the end quite appreciably out of pocket for the repair of that roof, and all the ornaments below that got broken in the process. And so it is in the 20th, as in the first century. The more you pray for people, the more your eyes are opened to their needs, and the realisation that, given the willingness, you yourself are probably in some measure in a position to relieve them. It may not be much you can do, but it is a comfort to remember that there was once a woman whose heart was moved, as it were, to intercede for Christ himself in his dangerous course, and anointed him lovingly and extravagantly with priceless unguents: an action which drew forth the best of accolades: 'she has done what she could'.

Use of the Body

The other problem raised was the part played by the body in prayer. All the great spiritual writers insist that each human spirit is led to God, and must be left free to be led by the Holy Spirit to God, by a different route. On the face of it this sounds absurd. The basic goals are so few: sight, obedience, union: how *could* there be more than a few well-trodden paths? But when we reflect that even the cells of our bodies are seen under the microscope to vary endlessly, so that no two even of these lowly mechanisms are the same, it is hardly surprising that so complex an entity as a human spirit, the pinnacle of creation, should prove unique in its needs, constraints, powers and destiny. By the same token, the relation of each human soul to the flesh in which it is embodied can hardly be taken for less than unique. In each case there is a working equation, and it is the equation which is unique.

Be that as it may, what we do with our bodies, outside as well as inside prayer, is of real moment. Alas, however, I have little of real moment to tell you, certainly nothing new. But perhaps I could begin with what is no more now than a faint memory of something said by St John of the Cross four centuries ago, something, which I remember surprised me in view of his ferocious self-detachment. He spoke of the nerves of the body being always present to consciousness, or something to that effect. We may begin, then, at least I feel I may begin by endorsing the view here expressed: continual awareness of the body, even though largely sub-conscious, is a fact, and one virtually insurmountable.

Our problem, therefore, is simply how to reduce consciousness of the body, by which I mean intrusive awareness, to a minimum. I suspect the best advice may be that of Samuel to Saul on a famous occasion 'do as occasion serves'; which at first sight looks like counsel for the lazy; but in retrospect, I would resist that conclusion. For years I assumed there was no other Christian posture but kneeling bolt upright. But two things tend to question this: fatigue, and the point St John of the Cross makes.

In the days of our youth kneeling upright may seem easy and invigorating; but even in youth there is such a thing as overwhelming fatigue, the battle against which may finally obliterate concern for prayer - (which makes it all the more astounding, to me at any rate, that so many nuns find it possible not only to remain bolt upright, but completely still and totally absorbed. This, incidentally, touches on my own personal problem: I can only remain still when relaxed, which is the reason why I seized on that remark of St John of the Cross with such surprise).

Wisdom, therefore, and more importantly, humility - by which I mean the courage to be different - and in particular to seem less holy than others, may suggest that more praying might be done in a posture that gives the body rest, and repose, and therefore reduces its intrusion into the flow of prayer to the minimum. But of course we have to be careful. If St John of the Cross has to be taken account of at one extreme of this consideration, Dr Pusey has at the other. For when consulted about this very problem, he committed himself to saying: 'it is plainly wrong to lean at prayer, when it could bring sleep'. (Spiritual Letters, 321)

But granted these two parameters, any posture is right which positively assists and facilitates prayer. Which may often mean that change of posture is also helpful, remembering another word of Pusey (306) to the effect that 'nothing makes prayer bad or good but perseverance and longing'. Kneeling is good, sitting can be good, lying on one's stomach can be right, so long as it brings us nearer to the One who is nearer than hands and breathing.

Dependence

Browsing recently, through the new Oxford Book of Prayer, I stumbled (on p.58) on an unreferenced piece of Newman, which I would like to read to you because it exemplifies, as perfectly as language can, what I mean by an attitude of dependence:

'Thou, O my God, art ever new, though Thou art the most ancient - thou alone art the food of eternity. I am to live for ever not for a time - and I have no power over my being; I cannot destroy myself, even though I were so wicked as to wish to do so. I must live on with intellect and consciousness for ever, in spite of myself. Without thee eternity would be another name for eternal misery. In thee alone have I that which can stay me up for ever: thou alone art the food of my soul. Thou alone art inexhaustible, and ever offerest to me something new to know, something new to love ... and so on for eternity I shall ever be a little child beginning to be taught the rudiments of thine infinite divine nature. For thou art thyself the seat and centre of all good, and the only substance in this universe of shadows, and the heaven in which blessed spirits live, and rejoice' - Amen.

Obedience

I have suggested that there are four vital clues lying about the world which will help to carry us over the gap between longing and its fulfilment in prayer; and all of these are located within the framework of the Body of Christ: the light of Christ in the eyes of fellow disciples; the exalting mystery of language; spelling out the mystery of Christ himself; the style of life, which is the life of Christ incarnated in his other friends and books.

However, there is another clue which is indispensable, and as it were the background, if not indeed the actual condition of our picking up these other hints: I mean the ongoing struggle to be obedient to the promptings of grace. Because, according to the fourth Gospel, Our Lord has attached a blessing to this which is *sui generis* and irreplaceable, namely the sense of his indwelling in the human heart, which is so strange as to be almost physical in its nature.

Indeed, it is this almost physical aspect of his indwelling which gives to Christian prayer one of its distinguishing marks: the fact that we do not need to call on God from afar, but, with infinite relief, need only allow ourselves to subside into the infinite depths which have somehow come to establish themselves in the ground of our being, a theme very central, as you know, to so much of Augustine.

And it has a further consequence of prime importance: it has much to do with the business of what the old books used to call recollection, or what St John of the Cross called 'a general, confused and loving attention to God'. The presence, facilitated by growing obedience, is basic, like the warm currents of the ocean: what is thus basic and semi-conscious rises to the immediacy of consciousness in the act of prayer.

Listening in Prayer

The assignment I was given for this morning, Prayer and Listening, is more complex than it sounds, for, as every priest knows, there is infinite scope for illusion and error in the kind of listening in prayer practised by so many of their more devout parishioners, often with such bizarre effects on both conduct and belief.

I am not denying for a moment that the listening ear is an essential to the practice of prayer. Indeed, if this paper were to have a text, it would be that moving verse of Ps 85: 'I will hearken what the Lord God will say concerning me; for he shall speak unto his people, and to his saints, that they turn not again'. All I am concerned to warn against is the idea that it is possible to enter into one's closet for the purpose of prayer, with the simple assurance that one will emerge by and by with a clear conviction of a solution to the problem on hand. I believe the business of guidance is more complex than this.

And I believe the nature of the complexity is indicated in that verse of Ps 85. For you will notice that though it opens with intense concern with and concentration on the self - 'I will hearken what the Lord God shall say concerning me', - *me* the way it continues instantly putting the word expected into the context of the people of God, the holy common folk, the *sancta plebs Dei* - 'for he shall speak peace to his people, and to his saints, that they turn not again' - a sentiment picked up in the N.T. dispensation by the powerful statement in 2 Peter 1.20 to the effect that 'no scripture is of any private interpretation', to which the NEB gives a particularly homely twist by translating it as 'no one can interpret any prophecy of scripture by himself', for, as Paul says in I Cor. 14.32, 'the spirits of the prophets are subject to the prophets'. (Would that the members of the laity, who are now plugging the gift of prophecy as the great new thing, could remember this).

So the initial point I am trying to establish is that whatever is whispered by the Lord God into the secret ear in the most private closet is ultimately of the nature of public truth, or what Maurice Cowley has called 'public doctrine' - though this is not to deny that what He says can in the first instance only be uttered in the most secret ear in the most secret place, if it is to have its maximal impact. The Lord who is the Spirit is always first and foremost the Lord of the whole Church. Yet truth, if it is to grasp us, and change us, and maybe through us change others, has to be uttered like this, so that it is received in the first instance as of the nature of actual revelation. Only in retrospect do we rise, or are we raised, to a perspective in which we are able to see it as part of a revelation which is also general, and part of the ancient faith; indeed, our appropriation of it can only be fully effective if so seen, as a particular application to the minutiae of our circumstances and cast of spirit, of what must hold good, for the whole community. All revelation has this public reference: witness the supremely public reference of the most secret salutation of Gabriel to Mary.

So, if I am right about this, we have to find a working context or framework within which the Spirit's secret whisperings can be received, contained and interpreted. And I would say that the outer shell of this public framework is the mystery of our God-given circumstances, starting with the huge basic fact of our creatureliness, and the consequence of this, our receiving of existence from moment to moment, from the hand of God himself, upholding us in this existence each created moment. Much has been written of late about the essence of being a Christian; but whatever else is left out, we can never exclude the urgent sense of invitation which meets us in the moment of waking, and holds us in its grip till the moment of collapsing back on the pillow; a sense of invitation calling us to follow the leadings of a holy and loving will through all the windings of a day, a day, which, as Anthony Bloom said, comes straight from God's hand - in such a way that whenever we are obedient we have a sense of light and peace, meaning and fulfilment, and contrariwise, contradiction, lostness and futility when we rebel and go our own way. Without this quite basic sense of ongoing dialogue with the living God in the interstices of the working waking day, no other, deeper, more secret and substantial revelation is possible or could be meaningful. Indeed, experience seems to suggest that all such deeper and more intimate revelation is by way of extrapolation of the more general background dialogue. And by dialogue, incidentally, I mean a very special conversation in a secret code language between God and each human spirit. Wordsworth used to say 'in the mountains he did feel his faith', i.e. mountains and cloud formations were code messages from the Divine. In the same way, for the Christian, events, and their peculiar cast and twists, are a code language for the heart, in the particular sense indicated in that verse of Ps. 64: 'all men that see it shall say, This hath God done; for they shall perceive that it is his work' – certainly *we* say it, if not all men. Each of us knows by a deep instinct what the Lord God is saying to us and concerning us through the private events of our lives, partly by their timing, often so breathtakingly right, by their severity, equally breath-taking, or their mercy, often tear-jerking, or whatever. Events for the Christian are like clues of an old crook to a trained detective: unmistakable signs: 'that man again', or 'the lovely man', as Farrer once called him, bringing mercy, discipline, joy and salvation. This, my point is, is the general background commerce with divinity, against which the deeper revelations of prayer have to be set and evaluated.

But I would maintain that for the thinking Christian there is an intermediate stage of dialogue between events and prayer, more specific than the language of events, and less specific than the language of prayer, namely, the ongoing ingestion of scripture. For here is what Blake called 'the great code', in whose silent mirror not simply private, but public events also, are interpreted as the voice of the living God, the high and holy one flying upon the wings of the wind, whose voice is yet heard not simply, or even mainly in the wind and earthquake, but most intensely in the still small voice; the high and holy one whose dwelling is with the meek and the contrite. We have, after all, just emerged from a very concentrated reading of the eschatological teaching of Jesus about the interpretation of events, so I needn't labour the point.

But I believe we are now in a position to understand a little more of what listening to God in prayer, i.e. private prayer, can mean. For prayer in this sense is not an out-of-the-blue activity, a superstitious drawing of lots or looking at the entrails of birds, but rather the regularly repeated period in which the awareness of the dependent creature, which is general and half-conscious in the savouring of events and more conscious in the elucidation of scripture, suddenly rises to its maximal intensity of consciousness, when the veils between are withdrawn, and we are involved in what Dionysius the Areopagite called 'a dim yet direct perception of God', in which the divine presence is perceived as what Bishop Hedley over a century ago called 'a spreading silent sense of something vague in outline, colourless and dim, accompanied by burning love'.

In this state the whole passion of the soul is released in an act of love meeting the grace-giving love which brought it into being; and when this happens nothing less than union takes place. This means, in the language of St John of the Cross, that 'a substantial touch' takes place between God and the human spirit, or as Jesus put it, he comes to sup with us, and makes his abode with us. Yet it is just here, where all seems so simplified, that the business of listening becomes most mysterious, for there is a lightning swiftness about the intimations of Divinity so great that, just as Moses could only catch a fleeting glimpse of God's vanishing back, so all our converse with God is in the nature of an afterthought. It's a bit like falling in love: the thing is so swift, we know that it has already happened, not that it is happening. We wake up to the fact that something has been said, spoken, uttered, in the depths of the soul, rather like that mysterious 'ping' that comes each week, which we know by instinct contains the substance of our next sermon, but whose verbal content requires days of thought, living, reading and prayer to elucidate.

It's a bit like the raw food which is brought to the basement tradesmen's entrances of those palatial mansions in Kensington without the owner's awareness, and which is served up days later in the shape of digestible meals. What is spoken formlessly, without voice or words, in the secret ear, is slowly articulated by the sensitive conscience, - sensitized, that is, by the habit of prayer itself - in terms of rational knowledge.

But, to end where we began, all such articulation, or realisation, is carried on within the context of the Body of Christ, every intimation being compared, tested, measured by his general word to the whole church, in scripture, in the ongoing life of the Church itself, and by the living wisdom of our brethren who are Christ's carriers and disguises. 'I will hearken what the Lord God will say concerning me, for he shall speak peace to his people, and to his saints, that they turn not again'. 'No scripture', nor any word of the Lord in prayer, 'is', or can be, 'of any private interpretation'. Its final validity, however intimate, is in the extent to which it produces humility and builds up the Body of Christ.
